WELP

WELP

Climate Change and
Arctic Identities

Michaela Stith

NEW DEGREE PRESS

WELP

Climate Change and Arctic Identities

ISBN

978-1-63676-849-6   *Paperback*
978-1-63730-193-7   *Kindle Ebook*
978-1-63730-293-4   *Digital Ebook*

To my international friends

*Anna, Nora, Chilon, Ole-Ante, Eben, Michelle, Susie,
Marja, Ture-Biehtar, Matta, and Gummi*

And my immediate family

Andrea Lynne, Treniyyah, Lili, Michael, and Christian

CONTENTS

———

AUTHOR'S NOTE

I've been given a few nicknames in my life: "Alaska," "Mother Nature," even "Mocha Mix." From birth, my mixed-race family took me fishing, hiking, and camping in Alaska. I adored sitting around the fire with my family eating freshly grilled Russian River salmon, picking wild northern blueberries from the hills around Anchorage, and waking up at four in the morning to ride my dad's huge 4x4 to the boat dock. I remember his strong arms hoisting me to his chest while he clapped and sang, "I'm Black and I'm proud!"

My life drastically changed when my dad passed away. At his funeral, the two hundred people in attendance said his smile could light up a room. He was brilliant and kind, but he struggled with addiction and depression. When I was on spring break during sixth grade, my dad took his life while surrounded by law enforcement. Alaska has some of the highest per-capita rates of suicide, substance abuse, police brutality, gun deaths, and violent crimes in the country, and—damn it *all*—too many of those trends impacted my own family.

When I talk about my dad's death, people seem to think it's shameful. "Do you really want to talk about that here?" they ask. Sure, it is excruciating for me to talk about it with people who don't understand systemic oppression. But I don't think his personal struggle is shameful; for me, too many people experience my dad's same hurt to believe it's *all their fault*. Even from a young age, I knew something was wrong with our government if it not only allowed but sponsored so many people's suffering.

As a seventh grader in Mrs. Ingland's geography class, I was assigned to write a travel brochure for any country in the world. I chose to write about Iceland: Iceland had had no murders in the last decades, few people in jail, and more examples of equality. Iceland's snow-capped volcanoes and lichen-laid landscapes reminded me of home. If equity could be achieved in other parts of the Arctic, why not at home? My education had always challenged me to reimagine what our world could look like.

Since before my dad passed away, schools funneled me from one gifted program to another. Anchorage is a statewide hub, built on Dena'ina homelands, and the most diverse city in the country with over one hundred different languages spoken in our school district. Isolated in nearly all-white classes, I lived a life of relative privilege. I learned how to talk and fit in—to hide my vulnerabilities from others—but I was always the butt of jokes about race and class. My teachers told us we would be the leaders of the next generation, but these students did not and could not represent Alaskans across the state. At some point in school, I decided I would have to be part of breaking down and making better systems of governance, from the inside out.

In college, I took advantage of all the opportunities Duke University had to offer: I lived in Iceland, visited Greenland, had amazing internships, protested racism on campus, and made friends from all over the world. I intentionally traveled back to Alaska every summer to wash showers and hand out clothes in a soup kitchen, canvass for environmental NGOs, help build resume-writing and job skills programs, and take notes at tribal meetings. This was on the university's dime because (guess what!) these adventures are affordable for almost no one.

As a young adult, memories with my dad on the land were one reason why I chose to study environmental science and policy. I learned that the Arctic is warming at double the global rate, and human activities had created a new phase in Earth's history: the Anthropocene.[1] It became clear to me that racism and environmental change were both wrapped up in colonialism and white supremacy. I remained focused on the ultimate goal of making Alaska a better place and, when I graduated, that passion landed me funding to work abroad in Norway through Duke's Hart Leadership Fellows program.

I worked in international policy administration six hundred sixty miles above the Arctic Circle in Tromsø, Norway/ Romssa, Sápmi, following the direction of Indigenous Peoples' organizations from across the North. I rode four-wheelers with reindeer herds in Guovdageaidnu, Sápmi, climbed tundra-clad mountains on Senja Island, and volunteered as a security guard at music festivals. I sat around the table with foreign ministers and secretaries of state from the eight Arctic countries, occupied the same conference building as President Vladimir Putin in Moscow, and proofread the Sixth Arctic Leaders' Summit Declaration, which highlighted Indigenous peoples' visions for the future.[2]

---

1   See the Glossary in the back of the book.

2   Aleut International Association et al., *VI Arctic Leaders' Summit Declaration* (Roavvenjárga: Arctic Council Indigenous Peoples' Secretariat, November 13 – 15, 2019).

Some people have called me a "very important person," to which I responded, "No, I work for very important people." Ultimately, I wanted to be useful to Indigenous leaders in their political work. It was Indigenous leaders who got the Alaska Equal Rights Act passed back in 1945, which benefited all of us in Alaska.[3] And they continue to drive justice movements in the state and the larger Arctic.

People like me—who only live in cities, fly country to country, organize meetings and administrate out of offices—don't understand the environment in the intimate way people who live in one place and steward it do. While Indigenous people make up only 5 percent of the world's population, they protect 80 percent of its biodiversity.[4] That kind of stewardship doesn't look like national parks supported by scientists and nation-states; it looks like hunting, herding, fishing, and trapping with place-based knowledge and traditions passed through generations and over millennia.

Many people believe technical solutions and political reforms can potentially solve our biggest problems: climate change, institutionalized racism, and economic injustice. The problem is, consumption and economic growth are core tenets of the American culture and mindset. Decision-makers often need a college education and a master's degree to work in places like the US Fish and Wildlife Service, and only 13 percent of Americans have those qualifications.[5] The people

---

3   Matthew Wills, "Alaska's Unique Civil Rights Struggle," *JSTOR Daily*, March 26, 2018.

4   Steven T. Garnett et al., "A spatial overview of the global importance of Indigenous lands for conservation," *Nature Sustainability* 1 no. 7 (2018): 369–374.

5   America Counts, "About 13.1 Percent Have a Master's, Professional Degree or Doctorate," *America Counts: Stories Behind the Numbers* (blog), February 19, 2018.

who make our country's policies don't live traditional ways of life and certainly don't hold that Indigenous knowledge about how to care for the environment. Those who want to curb climate change propose large, new renewable energy projects like wind and solar farms. Generally, they are relatively wealthy people who perpetuate cultural norms about consumption. Many environmental policies end up hurting, rather than helping, people who live intimately with the environment.

Here's the thing: You don't know what you don't know. I rely on guidance and friendships with people all around the Arctic. After reading this book, I hope decision-makers, activists, and all the people trying to figure out what to *do* to make a change in the world, think critically about their own world views. Gain a higher respect for lifeways and people you don't know much about.

Similarly, I want everyone who reads this book to come away with reformed visions of the North. I learned in my travels that most southerners think of the Arctic as a barren, icy wasteland devoid of people and filled with polar bears. When people look at rural regions as "empty," they distance those places in their minds. In the western mindset, wilderness places become something to be developed (for oil rigs, wind farms, mines), conquered (for summiting mountains, claiming property, and homesteading), or objectified (for science, political movements). Over four million people live in the Arctic. They have homes, use cars, guns, and phones, and even if they didn't, it's not acceptable to call people "primitive" or "backward." Indigenous people still live more sustainably and with fewer carbon emissions than Americans in the south. Not only five hundred years ago, but right now. Erasure of Indigenous people in both media and minds, as well as the notion that only wealthy, formally educated or powerful people have meaningful ideas, allow society to continuously neglect the harm it forces on Arctic peoples.

Equity must be accomplished on a cultural level, beyond political mandates and reform. As western people, some of our culturally ingrained beliefs are what created climate change, biodiversity loss, mass incarceration, and police brutality in the first place. Our knowledge systems are not enough to make the world a better place. We each need to learn about and develop relationships with the places in which we live and grew up. Being raised in Alaska, living in Norway, and traveling across the Arctic, I was able to view American culture both from outside and within. I believe it is time for us to realize that racism, environmental harm, and our systems of governance can inevitably be linked by one thing: white supremacy.

All the characters in *Welp* have had to see themselves through the gaze of white folks at some point and, because of white supremacy, this view was not always objective or positive. In this book, I show how a standard of whiteness in environmental decision-making undermines opportunity, security, and identity for dark-skinned and Indigenous peoples in the Arctic. If we are to make culture shifts that combat environmental injustice, emerging leaders will need to stand firm in their identities and worldviews. *Welp* is an opportunity to define myself in my own eyes, and for some of my closest friends and inspiring young leaders in the Arctic to do the same. Together, our narratives show that a brighter future for the Arctic can be possible when *we* determine the policies and decisions that affect us.

1

SUMMER I

SUMMER I

CHAPTER 1

EKSOTISK

If you have come here to help me, you are wasting your
time... But if you have come because your liberation
is bound up with mine, then let us work together.

—LILLA WATSON

"I can remember the first time I ever saw a Black," Bjorn
Christen said.

The hairs stood up on my neck. I wanted to leave, but his
eyes were locked on me, telling the story for my sake.

"It was quite creepy, actually," he continued. "Someone
knocked. The clock was around 22:00, and we never locked
the front door back then. It was dark, so I could barely see
him blocking the open doorway."

Bjorn Christen's monotone cadence revealed a small-
town North Norwegian dialect, but his mocking confidence
reminded me of white men I met in America. The silver hairs
of his eyebrows arched up on his forehead. His blue eyes
opened wide when he said, "He looked like Cheshire the Cat.
In the darkness, all I could see were his white teeth and the
whites of his eyes."

He chuckled. I glanced at the unaffected Norwegians around us and found myself alone.

Six hundred and sixty miles north of the Arctic Circle, I stood in a modern industrial-style lobby among mostly middle-aged professionals in an office building called *Framsenteret*, Fram Centre. I spent my weekdays working there at the Indigenous Peoples' Secretariat in the Arctic Council Secretariat office. *Framsenteret* hosted dozens of conferences and events year-round in Tromsø, Norway, mostly focused on climate policies and environmental science.

This October evening, scientists, interdisciplinary researchers, and fishing experts milled around *lysgården*, the roofed courtyard. The open space vaulted from the concrete lobby floor to the sunroof, surrounded by seven stories of offices on all sides. Architects built this part of the newly renovated office building ninety centimeters higher above sea level than the original coast-side building because, back when the building opened in 1998, most scientists couldn't imagine how fast the Arctic sea ice would melt in future summers.[6] Wearing my work slacks and a blue blouse with a bow around the neck, I had searched the crowd for familiar faces, sauntered over to the black-tied waitress, and ordered a *gratis hvit vin* (free white wine) with my *bong* (drink) ticket at the bar. I'd only been in Norway for two months, but I quickly learned that names for alcohol were quintessential vocabulary.

Receptions like this one happened in the lobby outside my office a few times a season. My colleagues raved I was more skilled at networking than they could expect for someone my age. At twenty-two, I was the same age as the Arctic Council,

---

6   Thomas Nilsen, "Expansion of Tromsø's Fram Centre makes room for more Arctic research cooperation," *The Barents Observer*, August 24, 2018.

the leading intergovernmental forum for Arctic states and Indigenous peoples to coordinate on issues of sustainable development and environmental protection in the Arctic. I still felt uneasy showing up at an event by myself.

Sipping my drink in the corner, I recognized Bjorn Christen's silver-blond ponytail and Harry Potter glasses from a workshop earlier. He was a renewable energy expert running feasibility studies in the North. I joined the group around him and introduced myself. I told them I was American, they asked how I was adjusting, and I confessed I still felt like I stuck out everywhere I went.

"Norwegians get excited about new types of people," one of them mentioned. "You are, you know…"

"Eksotisk," I finished.

I already knew what they would say; I'd heard how *exotic* I look a million times since arriving in Norway. Sometimes people exited stores just to watch me walk down the street. I started to braid my hair down so I wouldn't attract so many stares.

Immigration is fairly new to Norway, so many Norwegians aren't used to "different." There are ten times more immigrants in Norway today than there were fifty years ago, from about fifty-nine thousand in 1970 to nearly one million immigrants and Norwegian-born children with immigrant parents in 2020.[7] Nowadays, about 18 percent of Norwegians have an immigrant background.[8]

In Oslo, I had seen a crowd of Norwegians screaming at a brown man for riding his scooter too fast in the street. He

---

7   Norbert Beckmann-Dierkes and Johann C. Fuhrmann, *Immigration Country Norway—Demographic Trends and Political Concepts* (Berlin: Konrad-Adenauer-Stiftung, 2011).

8   Statistics Norway, "Immigrants and Norwegian-born to immigrant parents," March 9, 2020.

zoomed through the little cobblestone alley, collided with a white Norwegian girl who flew over her bike handles onto the ground, and caused twenty people on the crowded street corner to stop dead in their tracks. The two Norwegians with me stood and watched the whole dramatic scene to make sure the sobbing girl was okay. Two or three people hoisted her off the cobblestone. The man zealously apologized while an older woman chastised him like he was the five-year-old son holding her hand. Others joined in until multiple manicured index fingers wagged at him from every direction.

"I feel so bad for her," my friend lamented.

"I feel bad for the man getting yelled at," I retorted.

I'd seen colleagues call the taxi company to complain when—and only when—the driver was dark skinned. I'd heard of Norwegians who openly said, "Black people scare me."

I imagined a house full of Bjorn Christen's family yelling at the poor man to get off their property. The Black man on his porch was probably a delivery man from Posten, a religious missionary, or, at worst, someone new to town who stopped to ask for directions. But all Bjorn Christen had seen was the color of his skin—a novelty that struck fear into his ten-year-old soul.

After his story, silence fell over the group. Classical music and chatter saturated the background. I clicked my fingernails, unwilling to dignify him with a response.

"I remember my first Black also," offered another person. She sought my gaze, too zealous to tell her story. I floundered, ready for a way out of this discussion.

"Just for future reference, it's not very acceptable to say 'Blacks,'" I managed to tell them. They gaped at me.

"I only say what I read on the internet," Bjorn Christen protested, eyebrows furrowed. He seemed puzzled at my offense to his word choice, since American media freely used the term "Blacks" instead of "Black people." But what really offended me was the way Bjorn Christen talked about the first Black person he met. The outlandish description was different, if not less than human.

I lowered my eyes, excused myself from the conversation, and brought my wine glass to the six-story tall window at the backside of *lysgården*. At times when Norwegians made my cheeks turn hot and my fingers tremble, I liked to look outside at Tromsø and pretend I was still home in Alaska. Both landscapes boasted angular mountain ranges, birches and crowberry bushes, and animals like moose and halibut. Tonight, white caps peaked on the gray ocean and seagulls clamored over the water. The sky was heavy with moisture, and the wind continued to push clouds over the horizon. In my childhood, many perfect summer days were characterized by clouds, drizzle, and a cool fifty-five-degree temperature. Since Anchorage spring was an icy, slushy mess, and fall was a stormy cold, the brink of a summer rain shower became my favorite weather.

Yet Anchorage and Tromsø couldn't have felt more different to me. Over one hundred languages are spoken in the Anchorage School District, like Hmong, Yupik, Tagalog, Sudanese, Spanish, and Samoan. The city is overwhelmingly white—about two-thirds of the population—but the remainder manifests every color of the racial rainbow: 6 percent Black, 9 percent Asian, 3 percent Samoan, 6 percent Latinx, 9 percent Alaska Native.[9] Other than Hawaii, mixed-race people like me are more common in Alaska than any other state.[10]

---

9   World Population Review, "Anchorage, Alaska Population 2020," accessed January 9, 2021.

10   Julia O'Malley, *The Whale & the Cupcake: Stories of Subsistence, Longing and Community in Alaska* (Anchorage: Anchorage Museum, 2019), 5.

I remember hearing Samoans playing the ukulele (*oo*-ke-le-le not *you*-ke-le-le) as I roamed the hallways on my first day of high school. Over one thousand students watched Hawaiian girls perform hula at a pep rally, then I ate plantains at my Dominican boyfriend's house after school. I used to sneak out to parties at hockey players' houses with my Scottish-Jewish best friend, then drool over the Filipino boys at the breakdancing cyphers. At a friend's birthday who was Yupik and Aleut, we ate fry bread and ice cream made of Alaskan blueberries and cold seal fat; at a Korean friend's party, we ate pork belly Korean barbecue. Unlike re-segregated schools across the USA, West Anchorage High School was teeming with people of all races from all over. In fact, West was the fifth most diverse high school in the United States (following Bartlett and East, which are also in Anchorage).[11]

"Ahem." I glanced over my shoulder and found Bjorn Christen with a glass of wine in his outstretched hand. I had downed mine at the end of our last conversation.

He ended up sitting next to me at a dinner, where he argued for twenty minutes that cultural appropriation is just a compliment. When I told him Norwegians and white Americans have the privilege to get praise for wearing the same styles and showing the same behaviors that Black, Indigenous, and other people of color get racially profiled, harassed, and arrested for, he insisted "someone your age wouldn't understand." He went on to explain why American "Blacks" shouldn't say the N-word if they don't want Norwegians to use it.

---

11   Niche.com Inc., "2021 Most Diverse High Schools in America," accessed January 9, 2021.

As a former debate captain who helped get the team to the Alaska state championship and the *only* person of color around, I debated. I engaged with Bjorn Christen because his world view, just like anyone else's, drives the way he moves through life. If I could change his mind, maybe he wouldn't bombard the next Black person he came across with such negative biases.

I told Bjorn Christen about my personal experience in Norway: When I wore my natural curls, Norwegians stared open-mouthed at me in the street. He responded with a disgusting smile, "That's just because men think you're pretty."

It was becoming clear that civil discourse wouldn't cure Bjorn Christen's bias. With a forkful of salad poised near his mouth, he studied my face.

"At the risk of sounding racist…," he began.

Never a good way to start a sentence.

"What race *are* you?"

He squinted at me, and I sighed. This is a question to which I'm accustomed. Loose ringlets spring from my scalp like giant DNA strands. My thighs have always been thicker, lips a little fuller than my white peers. My eyes and hair are a deep brown like espresso beans, but my skin tone is olive. I look somewhere between, "I knew she couldn't *just* be white!" and "Michaela? *Black*? Noooooo."

"My mom is white, and my dad is Black," I said.

"What! I thought for sure you were Indian." Bjorn's mouth dropped clear to the floor, and his eyes bulged.

I assumed he meant Native American. He knew from my conference name tag that I worked at the Indigenous Peoples' Secretariat, which is a support secretariat for six organizations called "Permanent Participants" that represent Indigenous peoples across the Arctic.

When I got my fingerprints taken to apply for a Norwegian visa, a hazel-eyed police officer took one look at me and checked "Native American" in the race box. You could only check one box, so I made him change it to Black. I've been told my great-grandma lived on a Cherokee reservation, but neither my parents nor I grew up with the culture. It's not my place to claim Indigenous heritage.

"I'm just mixed," I repeated.

"Then why are you here?" He continued to shake his head in disbelief.

When I finally got the chance to excuse myself from the table, grab my coat and escape to the house, I thought about that very question. I was the only Black person I knew of at Framsenteret. This was not the first very uncomfortable conversation I would have about my race and identity in Norway. *Why do I put myself through this?* was a more apt question.

The answer is that the Arctic Council is one of the most inclusive governance structures in the world. Indigenous peoples, Black people, and other people of color bear disproportionate effects of problems like climate change, mass incarceration, and poverty. Yet in many state and national governments, we have been excluded from developing the policies that affect us. Despite Alaska's diversity, my own state's decision-making bodies are overwhelmingly white. At the Arctic Council, Indigenous leaders speak at the same tables as state representatives. I was drawn to the Arctic Council because I believe solving the world's biggest problems will require governments to listen to people who are most affected by them, and act upon their recommendations.

In Alaska, climate change has drastically altered the Arctic landscape. As a child, I always expected snow by Halloween. I can only remember one year when there were less than a couple inches on the ground. My mom had to design our Halloween costumes to go over snowsuits; I was a very fluffy tiger one year and an engorged pumpkin the next. But in 2013, 2016, and 2018, there was no Halloween snow.

Just twenty years later, the Alaskan winters I remember are relics of the past. Compared to the 1990s, Alaskan snow starts sticking to the ground a week later and melts two weeks earlier than normal.[12] We hit new high temperatures all the time, and scientists expect the Arctic Ocean will have ice-free summers in less than twenty-five years.[13]

Yet Alaskans do not experience these changes equally. I always considered myself part of the big city in Anchorage. Our tallest building shoots twenty-five stories into the sky and 40 percent of the state's population lives here.[14] It is an urban center well-connected to southern supply chains. By contrast, many Alaskan towns and villages can only be reached by boat or plane. A gallon of milk might be twelve dollars and two pounds of hamburger patties cost twenty-three dollars, more than double what we pay in Anchorage.[15] Many towns don't have internet access, and households in towns like Utqiaġvik pay upward of $350 per month.[16]

Above the Arctic Circle, the majority of people get half or more than half their food from the community's seasonal

12   Jon Dos Passos Coggin, "New report highlights Alaska's last five years of dramatic climate change," *ClimateWatch Magazine*, October 15, 2019.

13   Warren Cornwall, "The average US family destroys a football field's worth of Arctic sea ice every 30 years," *Science Magazine*, November 3, 2016.

14   World Population Review, "Anchorage," accessed February 21, 2021.

15   Julia O'Malley, "Whale hunting in Alaska: Point Hope, the village caught between tradition and climate change," *The Guardian*, July 16, 2015.

16   Maija Lukin, "Arctic Resilience Forum: Broadband Connectivity" (lecture, Arctic Resilience Forum, November 11, 2020).

hunting, fishing and whaling.[17] For example, Inuit have sustainably eaten whales in the region for 13,800 years.[18] With a family whaling crew, they can safely turn a one-hundred-thousand-pound bowhead whale into sustenance for an entire community. Providing food from the land is crucial in a region where up to 90 percent of wage-providing jobs disappear in winter.[19]

Though the media's narrative about the Arctic might focus on polar bears alone, people's lives and livelihoods are also at stake. On paths that were previously navigable and stable, experienced hunters fall through dangerously thin ice and pass away.[20] Animal migration patterns have changed as a result of land use and climate change, forcing people in remote villages to use choose between food and other expensive commodities. Meanwhile, over forty villages in Alaska must be relocated due to coastal erosion and storm surges caused by sea level rise; in extreme cases, homes are already crumbling into rivers and oceans.

It might seem ironic, then, that the oil and gas industry dominates Alaska so heavily that 89 percent of our state's tax money came from the sector's revenues during my senior year

17   TemaNord, *SLiCA: Arctic Living Conditions — Living conditions and quality of life among, Inuit, Saami and indigenous peoples of Chukotka and the Kola Peninsula* (Copenhagen: Nordic Council of Ministers, 2015).

18   Arctic Research Consortium of the United States, "12 - Melting Ice & Thawing Permafrost," panel at Arctic Futures 2050, September 23, 2019, video, 9:00-11:45, featuring Maija Lukin.

19   Yaari Walker, "Expansion of Maritime Activity in the Bering Strait Region: Mitigating Existing and Future Risks," virtual lecture by the Wilson Center's Polar Institute, July 2020.

20   Arctic Research Consortium of the United States, "Arctic Futures 2050 Conference: Day 2," September 5, 2015, video, 12:13-14:24, featuring Maija Lukin.

of high school.[21] As a teenager in Anchorage, it seemed like plundering the environment was the only way to make a living in the state. The names of major oil companies adorned the donor wall of every school building, nonprofit organization, and public structure. I remember political candidates rallying our student body to vote for them when we turned eighteen, so they could "get the Arctic National Wildlife Refuge open for drilling once and for all!" One doesn't have to wonder very hard about which industry funded their campaigns; Alaska's government is intimately dependent on the oil industry.[22]

During my senior year of high school, I even interned at an oil company while enrolled in a Masters-level course called "Climate Change" at Alaska Pacific University. I quizzed colleagues about the company's contributions to global warming and interviewed the engineers on my floor about the chemicals that go into fracking. Most of them didn't believe rising temperatures around the world were anthropogenic, or caused by humans. *Well, obviously, the climate is changing, Michaela* (eye roll)*, but that couldn't be my fault.*

Climate change, first and foremost, is a cultural problem embedded in our connection to and use of land and water. I think if Anchorage residents admitted permafrost thaw, unpredictable weather, and glacial melt were caused by fuel use and development, they'd have to acknowledge that their own profession contributes to the destruction they see while fishing, hiking, and camping on the weekends.

When oil prices crashed in 2015, our petro-dependence left us in an economic recession. Large companies like BP

---

21   Department of Revenue, Spring 2014 Revenue Sources Book (State of Alaska, 2014).

22   David M. Standlea, Oil, Globalization, and the War for the Arctic Refuge (Albany: State University of New York Press, 2006), 43-72.

left Alaska, just as the buildings and infrastructure built in the 1980s oil boom began to start looking tired. The state and municipality kept cutting their budgets, and the number of people experiencing homelessness began to climb. We have consistently been a state with the highest rates of suicide, gun deaths, and accidental death in the country.[23,24,25] So in 2018, 2019, and 2020, Alaska lost population.[26] While our political situation seems desperate, leaving is not an option many Alaskans would even want to consider.

Policy matters. It shapes the types of jobs available in the area, the laws enforced, the programs that get funded, and the cultural expressions allowed. But people don't have equal access or sway among policymakers. For example, Alaska Native people are more than 4 times more likely to be incarcerated than white Alaskans, and Black Alaskans are 3.5 times more likely—not because they are worse people, which is an inherently racist notion, but because we have the least inherited wealth and privilege.[27]

Like a petri dish for bacteria, America's lack of basic rights around health care, education, and minimum pay cause crime. Per 100,000 Alaskans, 691 are in prison. America's national average is 696, but the national average in Norway

23 Kavitha George, "Early data shows Alaska suicide rate stays constant, overdose rates increase," *Alaska Public Media*, December 23, 2020. Craig Medred, "The deadliest state of all," Anchorage Daily News, updated September 27, 2016.

24 National Center for Health Statistics, "Firearm Mortality by State," Centers for Disease Control and Prevention, last reviewed January 7, 2021.

25 Craig Medred, "The deadliest state of all," *Anchorage Daily News*, updated September 27, 2016.

26 James Brooks, "Alaska's population drops for the 3rd year in a row," *Anchorage Dispatch News*, updated January 9, 2020.

27 Prison Policy Initiative, "Alaska profile," 2018.

is only seventy-four.[28] Countries like Norway also provide humane living conditions in prisons, which America does not guarantee, and offer government funding that provides opportunity throughout Norwegians' lives. And when it comes to climate change, the Norwegian government has been strong and efficient about reducing the country's emissions.

When I first arrived in Norway, I hoped I could learn the secrets to good governance there. Each of us have different world views based on the lessons we were taught as children and the experiences we have in life that affect the types of policies we would make.

As I navigated social life in northern Norway, I paid attention to my new friends' worldviews, their thoughts about race and ethnicity, and their relationships with the environment. To me, all these sentiments were connected by environmental justice.

Environmental justice is a tool to achieve equity *and* fight climate change. The field links my love for people, desire to be around nature, and existential need to break down the high walls around policy and decision-making. Environmental justice requires a focus on people's well-being, hand in hand with care for the environment. It also requires that we recognize the rights of Black and Indigenous peoples, even when primarily white environmental authorities cannot see that there is a problem.

So, why am I here? The answer I gave Bjorn Christen is one that continues to drive my work in the Arctic:

"I'm not Indigenous, so I come here understanding I know less than other people around me about the Arctic environment and justice problems in Alaska," I said. "I want to be useful in any way possible. I plan to focus on listening and hope to learn how to be a better Arctic citizen."

---

28 Ibid.

CHAPTER 2

BRUNOST

———

Ut på tur, aldri sur. (Out on a trip, never angry.)
—NORWEGIAN SAYING

Before leaving Alaska, I read all the travel books I could find about Scandinavia: *The Almost Nearly Perfect People, The Nordic Theory of Everything, The Social Guidebook to Norway* and more. They all made it clear that Norwegians were notoriously difficult to get to know. Traveling in another country, I could meet a stranger at a bar, on the train, or somewhere else in public, ask to meet a second time for a coffee or a meal, and develop friendships from there. But Norway is not like every other country. If I managed to strike up random conversation with a Norwegian stranger—which was unlikely—and asked that person out to a coffee or a meal, I probably lost my chance of ever seeing that person again.[29] I was determined to avoid such errors.

I prepared to make a coordinated attempt at international friendship. In the literature, authors suggested getting

———

29   Julian S. Bourrelle, "How to Get to Know Norwegians," *The Social Guidebook to Norway,* September 3, 2019.

involved in activities, events, and clubs. Sober Norwegians are quiet, practical, reserved, and self-conscious. Restaurant meals are for family and close friends only, partly because you couldn't buy a meal on the town for less than twenty dollars. (Except the six-dollar cheeseburger at Burger King, which was always packed like a New York City subway car.) Small talk with strangers in public places was generally considered rude, and only an American would smile at passersby around bus stops, sidewalks, and malls. Structured conversations that didn't revolve around very tangible, temporal subjects were forgotten as quickly as I brought them up. In organized activities, Norwegians finally had the freedom to introduce themselves—a *reason* to pop the quiet bubble.

One day after work, I took a stroll down Storgata, the Walking Street, because I didn't want to go back to my *kollektiv* (shared house) yet. I was lonely and I wanted to meet more people. I hoped, like in America, that someone might call out or ask for directions. My goal was to have a conversation with someone. *Anyone.* And maybe a friendship would come from that.

At the busiest plaza on the Walking Street, I wandered around *Tromsø domkirke* gaping at the view of Fjellheisen: a picturesque mountain across the water from Tromsøya covered in greenery, but already starting to turn yellow with autumn. The square had recently been renovated. Dozens of people traversed it in all directions, staring but never speaking. I almost didn't believe my eyes when a man in his twenties or thirties with ebony skin and an African accent caught my eye, walked in my direction, and waved at me. He beckoned, "Unnskyld meg!" Excuse me!

"Sorry," I said with an unnecessary curtsy. "Jeg snakke ikke norsk." I don't speak Norwegian.

"Ah, ok," he responded, eyes bright. "Do you have a moment?"

I broke out in the biggest smile. *A human, a potential friend!* I thought. I missed human interaction. At home I might not have stopped and given him the time of day. Here, I nodded vigorously and started the conversation.

He reveled about his home in the south. Water was sparse and untreated; children had to walk miles to the public water center, which took away time from their schooling. His family members had ended up with cholera and passed away from diarrhea. I gasped and asked him to tell me more, all the while imagining the future of our friendship: two traveling Black people, trying to make some impact at home and shrugging off the Norwegians staring fearfully at us…

"Would you like to donate?" he asked.

What?

"Would you donate to UNICEF?" He smiled a broad grin. "I am here in Norway as a volunteer."

I should have known it was too good to be true. No one starts random conversations in Norway. *Well,* I thought, *that was a nice conversation anyway.* Goal achieved.

To really build a friendship beyond structured conversation, it was critical to include alcohol or nature in your activities. The literature said both made Norwegians especially chatty and friendly.

Therefore, I signed up to volunteer at three different summer music festivals in northern Norway before departing the States. One thing about me is I treat everything I'm really excited about like a school assignment. I made to-do lists, read the books relevant for Norwegian friend-making, scoured the internet for clubs, festivals, and events, and created expense spreadsheets for the cost of food and travel. I learned about Riddu Riđđu, an internationally acclaimed

Sámi music festival, and RakettNatt, a Norwegian festival with nationally popular artists and international stars like A$AP Ferg. I filled out the online volunteer forms without much of an idea about what I'd be doing; the most important part was the opportunity to meet people, without having to pay over US $200 to attend.

I arrived in Tromsø late on a Thursday in July, visited the office on Friday, and promptly set out to the grocery store to purchase a few food items that would last the weekend while I adventured to the first music festival: Riddu Riđđu. True to Norwegian work culture, the office was nearly empty. One employee, Katerina, only came to help get me situated.

"Is everyone on vacation?" I asked her.

"The office will be mostly empty until August." She shrugged. In a tradition handed down from Norse seamen, Norwegians typically take three to four weeks of vacation in the summer months. They fly to Thailand or Florida to escape the drizzle and the overly aggressive seagulls dive-bombing the northern Norwegian skyline. Although Tromsø was only home to eighty thousand people, there were direct flights from TOS to the Gran Canary Islands twice per week. The workers on those Spanish islands off the coast of Africa often speak snippets of Finnish and Norwegian.

"Luckily it will be quiet in the office," she said. She had accrued six weeks of vacation and would not be wasting any more days in the office. I wondered if this was normal, and later looked it up: Norwegian law requires employers to offer twenty-five days paid holiday leave in addition to twelve *helligdager*, public holidays. If you have a baby, the government pays for up to twelve weeks parental leave at 100 percent salary levels; the law requires fathers alone to take fourteen weeks paid leave before the child turns three years old.[30] Meanwhile, America offers zero guaranteed holidays and zero guaranteed parental leave.

I confided that I hate working in quiet spaces. I need a basic level of background noise to be established, after which I can dive into whatever I'm working on. Once, in my freshman year of college, I sat in the common room writing a four-thousand-word essay while twenty-five other freshmen cheered and booed at the Duke-UNC game. My fingers clicked away while they toppled over chairs and screamed with their blue-painted faces. It was the most productive I'd ever been.

"Do you have any plans for the first weekend?" Katerina asked.

I told her about the upcoming Riddu Riđđu festival this weekend. When I posed the trip to my boss, she signed me up for Nuorat youth group in excitement. But before I could go, I needed dinner. Katerina pointed me to the best grocery store. There was a closer corner shop, but the aisles were cramped and the food selection smaller.

I trudged twenty-four minutes up a slight incline—perhaps the furthest I ever walked for groceries—and found myself in the height of downtown near the library. The urban streets were litter-free, and the sun reflected off every windowpane. Many of Tromsø's buildings boasted walls made entirely of glass, including the library. South-facing windows are critical in the North: we do all we can to soak in the ever-present light source during summertime. Although the sun sat high in the Tromsø sky from June until July, never going down, it disappeared over the horizon in November and wouldn't resurface until January. This was called *midnattsol*, midnight sun, and *polarnatt*, polar night.

---

30   David Smith, "What's It Like to Work in Norway?," *A New Life in Trondheim* (blog), Life in Norway, March 2, 2015.

I walked past the library and slipped into the sliding doors at Coop Extra, a Norwegian grocery cooperative present around Europe, when it occurred to me that I forgot to download Google Translate before leaving the office. I watched myself sigh and square my shoulders as I passed under the video monitor hanging from the ceiling. Although I reached for the iPhone in my pocket instinctually, I knew it wasn't yet hooked up for data in this country. I would have to navigate the Norwegian store without internet, so a simple pasta with cheese and veggies would suffice for the night.

The street-facing store was smaller than supermarkets in America, but big enough to spend hours squinting at Norwegian food names and guessing their English translations. Red plastic branding bordered the store walls and refrigerators, stocked full of everything. A bag of white rice: *ris*. A half-gallon of milk: *mjolk*. A half-gallon of kefir. *Is that milk too?* I picked up a bag of frozen broccoli: *brokkoli*. The pasta aisle was nothing less than what I would except at home; all the Italian names were the same. Norwegian was surprisingly easy to read.

I wondered if I was easy to read. It wasn't long before I noticed eyes trailing me around the store. People met my gaze every time I turned my head. As someone advanced toward me in an aisle, my first reaction was to lower my gaze. You know that awkward moment when you catch someone staring at you and you look away? Norwegians don't look away. They don't smile or say anything. Only a foreigner (likely an American) would do that. The staring wasn't threatening necessarily; it just made me *acutely* aware I didn't belong.

At one point another shopper bumped into me as he walked by. I turned around and muttered sorry, but he had already walked off. *Rude*, I thought. I was told later on it was a cultural misunderstanding. At home, I would've made eye contact, said sorry, and walked away. From what I was told, Norwegians are too embarrassed to say *unnskyld*, sorry; they'd rather avoid the whole conversation. If you bump into someone in a store, you must not say anything except "oi."

I searched for the cheese aisle. At first, I couldn't find it. I paced around the store's entire perimeter to no avail until my third loop around the store. I finally discovered an aisle of fridges at the back of the store filled with rectangular, plastic-wrapped blocks. *Maybe these are cheese?*

Tine was the most common brand, but also the most expensive. The blocks of (hopefully) cheese were about six-by-four-by-two inches, ranging in price from sixty-five to 110 kroner—eight to fourteen US dollars. I refused to pay that much for cheese. One half-block of *Gudtbrandost* (literally "Good Brand Cheese") in maroon packaging was the lowest price: forty-eight kroner. I pledged to use every last gram of that cheese.

After another nineteen-minute walk up a very steep hill, I arrived at my new house. In the *kollektiv* there were four bedrooms, one-and-a-half bathrooms and a shared kitchen and living space. In the front, another entrance led into a separate section of the house with three more rooms. There was also a *hybel*, a finished basement, around the back of the house. Because of local legislation meant to make housing more accessible, it's typical to build out separate living spaces and rent them in Tromsø. Tromsøya has the same area as Manhattan and its population is growing. Rent is not much better than in Manhattan, either; for a bedroom in a shared house, I paid more than $800 a month (and that was the cheapest room I could find).

All of my to-be housemates were either enjoying the Arctic sunshine or lying on a beach in the Mediterranean. I unloaded three meager items totaling fourteen dollars onto the kitchen counter. The electric stove top heated salted pasta water while frozen vegetables rotated in the microwave (my housemates later teased my daily and diverse use of the microwave was "so American"). I pulled a communal Norwegian cheese slicer from the drawer: a small spatula-shaped tool with a sharp aperture that produced even cheese slices from the blocks I saw at the store. I opted for a cheese grater instead, more fitting for pasta.

I peeled open the plastic wrapping and revealed the cheese inside to be a candy caramel color. Smooth and brown. *Strange*, I thought, and began to shred it onto a plate. After dumping the cheese, pasta, veggies, and community-owned seasoning in a bowl, I grabbed a fork and took my first bite.

Brown cheese is a special Norwegian creation that, in taste, is not actually cheese at all. When I finally googled "Gudtbrandost brown cheese," the internet warned, "Will be horrible if you expect cheese. Can be good otherwise." Brunost is manufactured by first simmering goat's milk until the milk sugars caramelize. The resulting flavor is similar to a semisweet caramel chew, and the cheese sticks to the roof of your mouth like peanut butter. It is not used in pasta.

"Welp," I muttered out loud. When there's nothing to be done about an unfortunate situation, I shrug my shoulders and say *welp*. The word alone usually cuts the tension.

The sweet and savory taste wasn't entirely unbearable. I took a photo and sent the food to my mom. Alaska was nine hours behind so she wouldn't answer for a while. I picked up all my dishes, put them away in the dishwasher and went back to my room to pack up for the music festival.

Now that I was connected to Wi-Fi, I read on the weather app that the festival grounds would stay around forty or fifty degrees

Fahrenheit. The warmest sweater I had was a woolen *lopapeysa*. It was a two-year-old gift from my host family in Iceland. I hadn't anticipated being able to afford my one: handwoven in the world's fourth most expensive country to live, they cost over US $200.[31] But after months of exchanging stories about American and Icelandic politics over the dinner table, my Icelandic host mom bought me a custom gray *lopapeysa* with a necklace of cream-colored hearts around the collar. I smiled as I rolled up the fibrous sweater and packed it in the backpack.

Building relationships with different people around the world was my favorite part of travel. I finished packing and began to journal about the friends I wanted to make in Norway when someone knocked on the door.

"Who is it?" I asked.

"Anna!" A high voice like jingle bells floated through the door, which was painted white like the rest of my room. The Norwegians A's in her name sounded like *ah*, rather than the hard American *a* and soft *uh*. "My mom"—the landlord—"asked me to bring you hanger-thingies for your clothes."

I got up and opened the door with a smile on my face. "Hi! Nice to meet you."

"Hi!" Anna's black eyebrows arched up high with her ecstatic smile. Her body language mirrored mine closely: earnest, adorable, and energetic. We were about the same height, too, shorter than five-feet, three-inches. In a ponytail behind her head, her shiny hair draped down between her shoulder blades; her chestnut-colored skin was the darkest I'd seen since landing in Tromsø. What I learned from my boss, who had checked out the house before I arrived, was

---

31   Haukur Már Helgason, "Iceland: The World's 4th Most Expensive Country," *The Reykjavik Grapevine*, January 22, 2015.

that Anna was adopted from India. Her mom was Norwegian, and Anna had lived in Norway her whole life.

The house I was staying in was Anna's childhood home. She rented a room here from her mom, while her mom lived in the brand-new house the family built next door.

"My mom made waffles!" Anna smiled effusively. "She wanted me to bring you some."

"Thank you," I exclaimed. Without baking soda, Norwegian waffles are thin like pancakes and slightly crispy on the outside. They're cooked in a waffle iron that presses the waffles into six small hearts. Four were stacked on a plate and covered in plastic wrap.

"Usually, we put jam and *brunost*... bro-own cheese," she said. "Do you know what that is? Sorry, sorry. My English is so bad."

"I actually bought some earlier today," I told her and laughed. "And I promise it's better than my Norwegian." I was practicing on an app but knew next to nothing. Although the working language at my job was English—and I knew people's English would always be better than my Norwegian—I planned to learn to understand Norwegian conversation by the time I left Norway. "How long have you been speaking English?"

"Wow, a long time. We start learning English in year three."

From the age of ten, most Norwegians younger are fluent enough to watch TV in English, speak it on occasion, or use it fluently.[32] Only small differences gave her away: the word "wow" sounded like "vow." Her mom only learned English as an adult, and therefore sent Anna to provide the waffles and hangers.

"But I still get nervous. I need to work on my number of words... What is that called?"

---

32   "How Widely Spoken is English in Norway?," How Widely Spoken, accessed January 10, 2021.

"Vocabulary?" I offered.

We chatted for a while. She told me that she lived right down the hall in the other room on my floor, though she spent a lot of time with her mom in the house next door. There were also two bedrooms upstairs. I lived in the small bedroom off the side of the living room/kitchen/communal bathroom area. I came to like that room because it caused me to bump into my housemates often. I became the most long-term resident; seven others cycled through the vacant bedrooms during my stay, which ended up lasting over a year minus one Norwegian-style summer leave, and Anna eventually ended up moving in with her mom next door.

All the residents were nineteen to twenty-six years old, mostly students at the Arctic University of Norway. Some were from northern Norway while others were new to the region. All of them, except me and a Latvian couple, were Norwegians. Oftentimes foreigners build whole lives in Norway without making Norwegian friends because it's so difficult to meet them in the first place. I was lucky enough to live in a house full of Norwegians.

"I have a roommate named Nora," she said. In my head I heard "Noo-ra." But when I addressed a post-it to "Noora" on the fridge a few days later, Anna laughed at me and told me the correct spelling.

It turned out Anna and Nora had just moved from Alta. With less than twenty thousand people, Alta was the second biggest town this far north. To them, Tromsø was the big city where they could go shopping and spend summer vacation.

Anna decided to move here right after high school finished. "I didn't tell anyone I was leaving," she said. "I just, *poof!*" She told me she avoided people from her high school in Norway, even checking their locations on Snapchat before going anywhere. Nora was the person Anna was closest with, and she came to live with her. Both were nineteen and ready for a change in scenery. They needed new friends.

"You'll meet her," Anna said. "She's more nervous than me to speak English."

Anna is bubbly and outgoing. Her nickname in high school was "Det lille extra"—*a little extra*—because she was more giggly and expressive than the other Norwegians. Nora, by contrast, was more quintessentially Norwegian.

We did meet by coincidence—co-ink-ee-dence, as Anna would say—a couple days later.

Nora and I ate breakfast together at the dining table in the living room. Very pale with pink, freckled cheeks and a sporty blond ponytail, she chomped on dry toast with *brunost*, the brown cheese. I introduced myself and Nora said hi, but she didn't say another word for fifteen minutes.

Nora would describe herself as practical. She was straight-forward. Underneath her sure exterior, though, she was constantly calculating the right thing to say. She didn't like people who didn't consider other people's feelings when they made decisions. She knew other people assumed she was mean or cold because she spoke so shortly, so she got nervous in social situations. I didn't get a glimpse of those deeper levels for months to come.

"We should plan to hang out," I suggested. Anna was very excited. Over the next few weeks, we took walks, ate dinner together, and binged Norwegian TV with English subtitles. It wasn't until I saw Nora speak Norwegian with Anna that her personality came out. I couldn't stop myself from giggling when I heard them argue. "Nei," Anna asserted. "Ja," Nora said. *Yes.* "Nei!" Anna squealed. "Joo-oo," Nora urged in a lower, firm voice. Finally, Anna would sigh in exasperation.

After Anna left, I brought the waffles to the kitchen, heated them up and pulled the Norwegian cheese slicer from the drawer. From the fridge I grabbed my fifteen-and-a-half-ounce block of brunost and *jordbær* jam, one with Anna's name on a sticky note. She said I should borrow it for Norwegian waffles. I spread the jam on a heart-shaped waffle first, then slid the blade across the cheese to place a perfect slice on top. When I took a bite, the waffle was warm and sweet. The taste of friendship almost made up for my failure of a dinner.

CHAPTER 3

RIÐÐU RIÐÐU

It is in collectivities that we find
reservoirs of hope and optimism.

—ANGELA Y. DAVIS

I grew up not knowing the differences between "race," "eth-nicity," and "nationality." This is because teachers during one-on-one meetings, my friends' parents at sleepovers, and strangers I bumped into at the store were all curious about my race. When I was a baby in a stroller, strangers approached my mom with, "She's so cute! *What* is she?"

People usually avoided asking, "What race are you?" A few times they asked, "What is your nationality?" The answer to that was obvious: I'm American. Neither my mom nor my dad knew specifics about the countries our ancestors came from. Of course, "American" was not the answer people were looking for.

More regularly, strangers would walk up to me at McDon-ald's, the bus station, work, or the grocery store to ask, "What's your ethnicity?" This phrase was polite; it said race without saying race. Eventually, ethnicity became synonymous with race in my vocabulary.

At some point in my adolescence, I began assuming if someone had not asked about my race by the second or third encounter, they were shy. I would bring it up just to ease the tension: "My mom is white, and my dad is Black, and anyway, this relates to the conversation because..." Like many Americans, racial categories were a lens through which I saw myself and the world around me. I had arrived in Norway without any conception of ethnicity. Only race.

I'll tell you right now: Race is a poor metric by which to measure social justice in northern Norway.

Two peoples have lived in what is now known as Norway for at least a thousand years: ethnic Norwegians and Sámi. Sámi people have lived along the northern rim of Europe and Russia's Kola Peninsula for time immemorial. If a Sámi person dressed in western clothes immigrated to America (and many have), they would not be considered anything other than white. Whenever I talk about Sámi people with Americans, the first question in their minds is racial makeup: *Are they like Europeans, or did they come from Asia?* We are programmed to use race to understand and categorize other people. In fact, no one has been able to trace the genetic origin of the Sámi people because "Sámi" is not based on race or genetics; it is a culture, an ethnicity.

From the 1920s up until the 1990s, the Norwegian government employed a set of assimilation policies called Norwegianization: "fornorsk." During fornorsk, the government took much of their land away, forbade everyone from speaking Sámi languages, burned Sámi clothes, mandated that Sámi schoolchildren move hundreds of miles away from their families for residential school, and forced Norwegian customs on them.[33]

---

33 Henry Minde, "The Norwegianization of the Sami - why, how and what consequences?," in *Sámi skuvlahistorjá 1*, eds. Svein Lund, Elfrid Boine and Siri Broch Johansen (Kárášjohka/Karasjok: Davvi Girji, 2005).

A group of Sámi leaders founded Riddu Riđđu at the tail end of that era; in 1991, a group of Sámi youth created an Indigenous festival in Kåfjord municipality—or Gáivuona, as it's known in Sápmi—where Sámi were free to celebrate their culture without shame.[34] The festival gathered emerging Sámi artists on old farmland.

Twenty years later, the Center for Northern Peoples was built on festival grounds, complete with a Museum for Northern Peoples focused on Sámi history. People traveled from all over Sápmi to attend the annual festival; many met their wives and husbands there. Over time, Riddu Riđđu became a gigantic affair. Hundreds of tents and *lavvus*—traditional Sámi tents—popped up on the festival grounds every July, with up to 9,200 people in attendance.[35,36] The festival gained outside attention and the organizers began to market the occasion as an international Indigenous festival, where people of all cultures were welcome.

I carpooled to Riddu Riđđu with a group of other volunteers. Although Norway looks skinny on a map, Troms Municipality itself is bigger than Maryland, and Finnmark to the north is even larger. From the passenger seat, I gazed over the treacherously narrow road at unending, unwavering vibrant fjords. The highways followed the curvature of the shoreline: hills and ridges sloped up to the right of me, while a flimsy guardrail promised to keep the car from falling into the sea on the left side. The water was so clear and turquoise

34 "Riddu Riđđu," Museum for Northern Peoples, Center for Northern Peoples, 9144 Samuelsberg, Norway, accessed July 11, 2018.

35 Kia Krarup Hansen, Turid Moldenæs, and Svein Disch Mathiesen, "The knowledge that went up in smoke: Reindeer herders' traditional knowledge of smoked reindeer meat in literature," *Polar Record* 55: 461.

36 Riddu Riđđu Festivála, "About Riddu Riđđu," accessed January 10, 2021.

that I saw yellow rocks on the seafloor from the far side of the road.

Travelers came to Norway for these views: the unending nature speckled with tiny towns and A-line roofed red houses, without the light pollution and tall buildings in populous cities like Oslo, or even Tromsø. When I started venturing further north into Sápmi and told rural residents I lived in Tromsø, they tutted and pitied me. Who could possibly *enjoy* living in a city?

When we arrived, I exited the car with a turquoise backpack on my shoulder, hiking boots on my feet, and a bright yellow sleeping bag in my arms. The Riddu Riđđu campground was deep green in full summer bloom: leafy green birches, vines ripe with tart, red lingonberries, short grasses alongside cold glacial streams rushing to the ocean. The flat valley marked where a glacier once sat, and rocky hilltops still packed snow into crevices on either side of the steep valley. Two white pyramid tents filled enough of the campground to each hold one hundred people for nighttime celebrations. My eye followed the smoke rising from the tops of a few fifteen-foot-tall *lavvus*, where firepits crackled inside.

Most festival goers were setting up their personal tents and *lavvus*. I planned to spend the night in the wooden school building near the Center for Northern Peoples with a couple dozen thirteen to twenty-five year olds. The youth group was primarily Sámi and included Indigenous people and people of color who flew from Russia, China, Taiwan, Finland, Norway, and Greenland. All the teen and young adult participants slept on air mattresses atop a classroom floor—girls in the fourth-grade classroom and boys in the fifth. I found my way into the fourth, where twin mattresses lined and stuck out perpendicular from the four walls.

"Er du klar for timen?" I turned around to see a blond young man, no more than twenty-one, asking me the question. He wore a 2017 Riddu Riđđu volunteer shirt and smiled big, more than anyone I'd seen so far. "Er du klar" was the first phrase the Norwegian language app had taught me—*Are you ready?* But the full meaning of his words still slipped my grasp.

"Andreas," the girl standing beside him scolded and wagged her head. Her round eyes shot him a pointed look as she turned toward me. "I'm sorry, Andreas knows we're all speaking English in Nuorat."

I blushed, but they weren't speaking English for my sake. This festival, including the youth group, gathered Sámi people from as far as the sloping hills in Kolksy District, Russia to the Sámi town where all roads meet, Guovdageaidnu. Because of assimilation policies, many of the youth didn't speak Sámi; their first languages were Norwegian, Finnish, Russian, or Swedish. For those who spoke their mother tongue, it was still very difficult for a north Sámi speaker to communicate with a Lule Sámi speaker. There are nine Sámi dialects and the furthest ones from each other are as different as Norwegian and German. Here, English was the most universal language.

The girl leader, Marja, informed, "There's a welcoming ceremony in the main *lavvu* down the road at 16:00. We'll all walk down together!"

Shorter than me with straight, blond hair down her back, she wore a summer *gákti* that she'd made with patterned cotton I might have bought at Michaels. It was a modern twist on the traditional dress, which fanned out at her waist to come to a swirling hem just below her knees.

In the hour before the welcome began, I followed Marja and some others toward the Museum for Northern Peoples with a pencil and notepad in hand. There was a breeze and slight drizzle as we walked down the valley from the school. I snuggled into the handwoven *lopapeysa* my Icelandic host mom gifted me, which never seemed to get drenched by water.

The entryway to the museum featured a road sign riddled with bullet holes. Troms county mandated bilingual signage in the last ten years, but the brand-new sign pointing toward Gáivuona was vandalized by local Norwegians as soon as it had been put up.[37] When it was replaced, the old one would be remembered on display. As I filed behind Marja to the exhibits downstairs, I hoped to learn more about Sápmi than I could find online.

Unlike Norwegian history, I could barely find factual information about Sámi before arriving. The most I found were basic definitions: Sámi are the only recognized Indigenous people in Europe. Their traditional homeland, Sápmi, stretches beyond northern Norway to encompass northern Sweden, northern Finland, and the Kola Peninsula of Russia.[38] I wasn't so interested in impersonal analyses that diminished people to study subjects. What did Sámi people have to say about their own history? Now *that* was worth knowing, and the museum exhibit gave some idea.

While we strolled through, I chatted with Marja and Ture-Biehtar, a very impressive seventeen year old from the Finnish side of Sápmi. Not only was Ture impressive in the gravitas and passion of his voice, but also that he was at least a foot taller than both of us girls and many Sámi people at the festival.

---

37   Florian Hiss, "Tromsø as a 'Sámi Town'? – Language ideologies, attitudes, and debates surrounding bilingual language policies," *Language Policy* 12, no. 2 (May 2013): 177–196.

38   "The Sami of Northern Europe – one people, four countries," United Nations Regional Information Centre for Western Europe, accessed January 10, 2021.

"Have you been to Riddu before?" I asked him, hushing my voice in the museum.

"I came once before," said Ture, with an unhurried and measured manner. He grew up outside Sápmi in a town in southern Finland, where his was the only Sámi family. "Riddu is a big party, but it's also a safe place where you can casually be yourself."

I tapped screens along the wall of the museum to illuminate their messages. Over millennia, Sámi developed knowledge systems that allowed them to thrive in an Arctic environment, even throughout the last Ice Age. In northern Sápmi, that meant caring for reindeer herds to produce food, clothing, and shelter. The interactive computer said reindeer-herding northern Sámi shared land collectively among their *siidas*, or family groups, traveling on foot and by sled between reindeer pastures. Close ties with family were always key to Sámi life. This was not new information for my friends.

On the Norwegian side of Sápmi, Marja's ancestors coexisted, traded meat for metals, and intermarried with Vikings for a long time. But under a new, Christian king, Norwegians were instructed to eliminate paganism and assimilate the Sámi into the king's property-owning system in the 1600s. One museum screen said the Danish-Norwegian King Christian IV terminated Sámi rights to land in 1608.[39] The state bought up Sámi land, giving Norwegians control over their subsistence activities toward the end of the century. Surveyors were sent to eliminate collective land use and impose strict punishments on Sámi for minor

---

39 "Svartskogen," Museum for Northern Peoples, Center for Northern Peoples, 9144 Samuelsberg, Norway, accessed July 17, 2018.

infractions, such as illegal woodcutting.[40] Sámi shamans were executed and their sacred drums were burned over time.[41] The Norwegians' Bible said the land was theirs to take, so they took it from Sámi by force.

To my surprise, the history of colonization was not so different in Norway than in the United States.

"What brings you all the way from America?" Ture-Biehtar asked.

I told him about my new job at the Indigenous Peoples' Secretariat, eager for my first weeks in the office. No, I answered, I was not Indigenous myself. My mom is white, and my dad is Black.

Marja's eyes flickered with curiosity. I noticed her cat-eye liner with glitter at the tear ducts. She was a college student excited to explore the world; she would study abroad in Central America next year and live with an Indigenous friend she met at Nuorat years prior. Still, her center was firmly rooted at home.

"My mom is Sámi, and my dad is Norwegian, but I am Sámi," Marja told me. "I don't think it makes sense to say I am half Sámi. Then if I marry someone who is not Sámi my children will be one-quarter Sámi... Eventually we would lose the Sámi people."

Ture was mixed too, and agreed with Marja: "blood quantum," a concept that the governments of Canada, the US, and others use to define Indigenous people, does not apply in Sápmi. Because of assimilation policies and, in Australia, forced interracial childbearing, genetics don't tell an

---

40   "The Surveyor Case," Museum for Northern Peoples, Center for Northern Peoples, 9144 Samuelsberg, Norway, accessed July 17, 2018.

41   Kimmi Woodward, "The Sami vs. Outsiders," *Sami Culture* (blog), The University of Texas at Austin, accessed January 10, 2021.

adequate picture of many Indigenous people's identification with their tribes.[42]

My own racial or ethnic identity felt out of reach during my adolescent years. In America, the one-drop rule kept Black people as property, regardless how many slave owners had inserted their ancestry in the bloodline. It continues to shape the way the country thinks about Blackness. From my own experience, though, I knew that Blackness was also conditioned on the way people perceive your race.

Among other people of color, I didn't have to prove myself. In middle school I had a core group of girl friends who were Indigenous, Latina, Asian, and white. We had all recognized what it was like to be the only ones that looked like ourselves in the classroom. At our middle school, the whitest one in Anchorage, less than ten of eight hundred students were Black. Mostly white children in my highly gifted classes called me an Oreo and argued with me when I told them not to say racist things. They almost took offense to my self-identification: "You're not even Black!"

Similarly, Ture said, "I knew I was Sámi, but I didn't realize it was an important part of myself until I was thirteen or fourteen." In upper secondary school, one of the bullies in school called him a *reindeer fucker*. Many Finns looked down on Sámi reindeer herders' deep knowledge about the animals. Ture had the choice of accepting the verbal abuse or fighting back. He fought back by being himself unapologetically.

We paused in the exhibit to reflect on the significance of being together. The deep brown wood floors and soft light had a kind of calming effect.

---

42   Philip Knightly, "Longtime *Australian Policy: Kidnapping Children from Families*," The Center for Public Integrity, updated March 19, 2019.

Ture remarked, "The festival is a great motivation to take a trip, talk Indigenous politics, trade experiences of racism."

"We can learn more about each other's lives," I replied. Somehow, our experiences seemed similar.

Ture told me later that his driving ambition was to get the ILO Convention number 169 on the Rights of Indigenous Peoples ratified in Finland and Sweden. Norway was the first nation to ratify ILO 169 in 1990, signaling the end of fornorsk. Finally, the state formally agreed to ensure Sámi people's right to further develop their culture.[43] Legally, Sámi in Norway should be able to control their own institutions, ways of life, and economic development, as well as maintain and develop their identities, languages, and religions.

While all Sámi have representative bodies in the Scandinavian countries where they reside today, the bodies are restricted by the laws in each nation. Ture would like to see a combined council among the Sámi in all four countries where they are present.

"Not having an impact on the world is something that I find terrifying," Ture said. "I would like to see real autonomy and equal human rights among Sámi."

"What inspires you to do this work?" I asked him.

Ture shook his hand through his hair. He told me his family members have maintained a culture of leadership in Finland: His sister was a leader in Sámi youth politics and his grandfather revived Sámi *duodji*—Sámi handicrafts—after their creation had been shunned in Inari. On his mother's side, his great grandfather was a general in the Finnish army and an assistant to the Secretary of the

---

43 Norwegian Ministry of Local Government and Modernisation, "The ILO Convention on the Rights of Indigenous Peoples," *Regjeringen*, February 20, 2020.

United Nations. His family legacy and lived experience both drove him.

"In a way, trauma enabled a path which I have later decided to take," he continued, speaking quietly. "I am a minority; these are facts of life. There is adversity associated with that. But, because of the perspective I have in myself, I am better at handling that adversity, recognizing it, and picking my fights, so to say."

Marja was also inspired by adversity to attend medical school. Riddu was one of the first events in her gap year, after which she would start studying medicine in 2019. Norwegian hospitals need doctors and nurses who can communicate with elderly Sámi, and they will pay a pretty penny if you have the skill.

"Many elderly Sámi—people who are over sixty now—had to give up their language when they were young," she said. "To protect their children, they never told their family they were Sámi. As they got older, a great number of these people developed dementia. They can only remember their first language: Sámi."

During fornorsk, the use of Sámi language was outlawed from 1870 to 1970. The government required that Sámi children attend residential schools, where they were forcibly separated from their parents, subjected to abuse, and taught children to be ashamed of their language and traditions.[44] Many people assimilated, never telling their children they were born Sámi.

Marja touched the computer screen, a little wistfully. The elders' children gained an identity they never knew they had.

---

44 Henry Minde, "The Norwegianization of the Sami - why, how and what consequences?," accessed March 25, 2021.

These parents and grandparents looked enough like Norwegians to convince everyone—even their own families—that they were Norwegian.

"Are there stereotypes about how Sámi people look?" I asked. I was used to skin color determining the way people move through society, but this went further than skin deep. I wasn't sure I could imagine the weight of that burden: the choice to give up yourself to survive.

"When I visited Oslo and I told people I was Sámi, they would say, 'No, you are not short with brown hair. You don't have small eyes. You can't be Sámi,'" she said, shaking her head. "But it is very difficult to say what Sámi look like because we are all very mixed."

Reindeer herders were nomadic, traversing hundreds or thousands of miles between summer and winter pastures. Reindeer herders today still have to move their herds between seasonal pastures.

Marja continued, "Yes, believe it or not, one hundred years ago people had sex too. Sámis would travel to follow reindeer herds and," she motioned her hands around, "Badabing! Sex with all different peoples."

"I get you," I said and laughed a little too loud. But Marja continued grinning back. Riddu Riđđu Festival was a place where we could laugh and be loud in public, and no one would question why. The museum's examples of adversities northern peoples faced also symbolized resilience: Together, Arctic peoples had been through a lot and continued to persevere. Sámi culture was worth celebrating.

By the time we headed down the hill, most young adults in my group had adorned in bright and shimmering *gáktis*. It was a dress on women or a tunic on men, cinched at the waist with a belt decorated in silver loops. Everyone I asked had either made their own gákti or someone in their immediate family had, so you could tell the region they came from. South Sámi wore gorgeous chest pieces with silver labyrinths on top of red-, green-, and blue-checkered backgrounds, while Sámi from the Russian side used tiny white beads to create patterns of mountains along their shoulders and collars, for example.

Ture chortled as he slid candy bars in the empty space in the shirt above his belt: "And it's great for storing food."

We all gathered in the gym for lesson one: how to dance *syddis*, a Sámi swing dance. The instructors were two young student leaders from the Sámi Pathfinders program who volunteered to travel around Norway and teach aspects of Sámi culture.[45] When we were told to find partners, young women grasped their friends' hands while awkward boys huddled in a corner. Ture and I paired off.

The instructor pressed play on her phone, and the ring of an accordion sounded around the gym. It followed with a guitar, bass drum, and a modern joik by the Sámi folk band, Felgen Orkester. With my right hand in Ture's left, poised just below our shoulders, we practiced the steps. Like a rocking chair, we leaned into our front feet, hopped onto our back feet, touched the ground behind us with our front feet, and stepped forward to begin again. I laughed when Ture confidently led me around the gym.

"You're a really good dancer!" I said, raising my voice over the lyrics. When the instructors paused the music, I clapped ecstatically.

They gave a few more steps to incorporate. Every step forward was a gigantic leap forty-five degrees counterclockwise. When we teetered backward, Ture kept us from falling over.

---

45   Samisk Veivisare, "About Sámi Pathfinders," accessed February 22, 2021.

If before we looked like a rocking chair, now we look like a rocking chair in a hurricane. And then came the turn, where Ture let go with one hand and I went spinning.

The court lines began to run together on the tan rubber floor. Dozens of us continued spinning around the room, glittering in the midnight sun and stumbling over each other's feet. I felt free and energized; after a few days of secluded quietness in Tromsø, this lively festival made me excited for the next months I would spend in Sápmi. Being fully immersed here was both a treat for me and a reservoir of joy and pride for my new friends. Although our ethnicities were different, we shared so many sentiments about embracing ourselves.

Ture said it best: "Choosing to be unapologetically myself and educating myself on my culture—which I might add, wasn't an easy task in a country that has whitewashed everything—has led me to see structural racism everywhere. It's not always good for mental well-being. The benefit of it, though, is that it enables me to be a better person. Because despite all the things I see around me, I decide to be kind; I decide to be better."

2

SUMMER II

CHAPTER 4

MØRKHUDET

In this country, American means white.
Everybody else has to hyphenate.

—TONI MORRISON

I learned how Norwegians conceptualize race from my house-mates. We occasionally spent time as a group, putt-putt golf-ing at Storgata Camping or taking walks around the wooded lake atop the island called Prestvannet (literally: "the priest water"). Most commonly, the four of us and other housemates sat around the hardwood-floored, -walled, and -ceilinged living room playing card games. One night during a game of twenty questions, I had a sticky note stuck to my forehead with a name on it and no clue what that name could be. When I narrowed down the subject to a female celebrity, I asked her race.

"Is she white?"

"Ummm, maybe?" they floundered. My eyes darted between each of their faces in hopes they would give me a hint. They blinked back at me, unable to answer. As my number of guesses ran out, I blurted names of all the racially ambiguous, white-ish people I could think of.

"Halsey?"

"Who is that?"

"Vanessa Hudgens? Mila Kunis? Adriana Lima?" No, no, no. Eventually I exhausted my questions. I peeled the sticky note off my forehead and read the name of the maybe-white female celebrity: *Cardi B.*

"Y'all set me up," I frowned.

Cardi B is a Black Latina. When accused of not being Black, her Instagram story response was, "My features don't come from white people fucking, okay?" Her parents' and grandparents' races are Black. Their nationalities are Dominican and Trinidadian.[46] Period.

I always lost these games. Norwegians have such a different way of conceptualizing American culture that, even if I knew the answers, we rarely understood each other. Race had so thoroughly shaped my family's experiences in Alaska, I was dumbfounded that Norwegians understood it differently.

When categorizing people, Americans think in terms of race: Black, White, Latinx, Asian, and Native American. We think that each race is supposed to have a way of acting and speaking. For example, we refer to "the culture" as in Black culture. The culture might include songs and dances you should know, skepticism for the police, the debate whether sugar or salt belongs in grits, and so on. There are some characteristics Black Americans use to define ourselves.

Race is your skin color and physical features. Your race itself doesn't biologically or genetically affect how you act or speak. If you're born Black in America, then get adopted by a wealthy Norwegian family before you can speak, and grow

---

46 Ny MaGee, "Fat Joe Talks Africa, Culture and Declares That 'Latinos Are Black'," Electronic Urban Report/EUR, September 22, 2019.

up as Norwegian, you will still have dark skin and textured hair. You just wouldn't have been raised with the culture. The mannerisms and customs we associate with race are called ethnicity.

Those feelings of identity are critical, because they allow you to be part of a like-minded community. For some, the fact that Cardi B speaks Spanish disqualifies her from being Black. Because Americans aren't taught to consider the differences between race and ethnicity, we conflate Cardi B's ethnicity with her race. In fact, Black people have *so* many different ethnicities: Muslims in Philly, cowboys in Texas, Dominicanos in New York, and the list goes on.

Meanwhile, Norwegians are taught about ethnicity. They know that a Norwegian—not a white person in general—must speak and act *just so* to be Norwegian. Norwegians know that they are white and Finnish people are white and so are Swedes, but things start getting a little unclear as you go further south.

"I used to think Greek people were Black," Susie told me, sticky note between her brown hair and blue eyes. In addition to Anna and Nora, Susie was my closest friend in the house. She was a twenty-three-year-old college student at UiT—The Arctic University of Norway and a fifth-generation Norwegian in Tromsø. The government had granted her great-great-grandparents a huge swath of land encompassing the entire visible coastline of Tromsdalen, the mainland part of the city.

Although many imagine Viking-descended Norwegians to be particularly tall and statuesque, Susie was fairly short with a short-bridged nose. She says her non-Norwegian features likely come from a Sámi great-grandparent and, as a child, she didn't like her nose. The shame Norwegians placed upon Sámi identity was so great that no one in her family could, or would, identify the Sámi ancestor. That part of Susie had been assimilated and lost.

Technically, Norwegian-ness is an ethnicity. It is about the language you speak, place you grew up, and cultural references you have. Yet small differences in racial features like slight upturns in the eye, high cheekbones, short nose bridges, and statistically insignificant differences in height are considered stereotypically Sámi. Norwegians, like Americans, are also guilty of conflating race with ethnicity.[47]

When someone with tan skin, dark eyes, textured hair, or hijab walks in the room, many Norwegians would automatically consider them *utlending*, foreigners. There's just one racial term to describe people who don't look Norwegian: *mørkhudet*, "dark-skinned." As hard as some *mørkhudet* people strive to be Norwegian, they will always need to prove their knowledge and mastery of the culture. Integration is emotionally—and sometimes physically—a violent process.

On Norwegian soil, the only terrorist attack in history was a solo Norwegian shooter who believed the government had unlawfully subjected ethnic Norwegians to mass immigration since the 1960s. He blamed the more progressive Norwegian Labour Party. On July 22, 2011, he killed nearly eighty people during attacks against the government office complex in Oslo and Labour Party youth camp on Utøya.[48] Some will never consider *utlending* or *mørkhudet* people to be Norwegians.

In America, we erase ethnicity with race. Are you Norwegian or Sámi? The moment you show up to Ellis Island and

---

47   Tony Sandset, *Color that Matters: A Comparative Approach to Mixed Race Identity and Nordic Exceptionalism* (New York: Routledge, 2020), 5.

48   "The 22nd of July 2011," 22. juli-senteret, accessed February 17, 2021.

are handed a census with the check boxes for race, it doesn't matter: *Congrats, you're white.*

We neglect, however, that American-ness is also attached to whiteness. Whenever I traveled to Europe, people commented, "You don't look American." Based on the composition of our Congress (78 percent white[49]), the leaders of American businesses, the number of non-white presidents, and the media we export around the world (think of the show *Friends*, or any 1990s–2000s rom-com), people assume an "American" is typically white, Protestant, and English-speaking. Domestically, we learn about the accomplishments and histories of white Americans in typical coursework, while "Black history" is relegated to a specific month.

Like *mørkhudet* people in Norway, Black Americans have to assimilate to whiteness to access the full benefits of American citizenship. We are forced into the debate on respectability politics: whether or not to conform to "mainstream," white-acceptable standards of appearance and behavior.[50] This is because, for example, job applicants with white-sounding names like Emily and Greg are called for interviews 50 percent more often than those with Black-sounding names like Lakisha and Jamal, even for the exact same resume.[51] This sort of racism is in the water, baked into subconscious biases and unchecked assumptions that make up American culture.

---

49   Kristen Bialik, "For the fifth time in a row, the new Congress is the most racially and ethnically diverse ever," *FactTank* (blog), Pew Research Center, February 8, 2019.

50   Damon Young, "The Definition, Danger and Disease of Respectability Politics, Explained," *The Root*, March 21, 2016.

51   Marianne Bertrand and Sendhil Mullainathan, "Are Emily and Greg More Employable Than Lakisha and Jamal? A Field Experiment on Labor Market Discrimination," *The American Economic Review* 94, no. 4 (2004): 991-1013.

When Black people in particular don't conform to laws made almost entirely by white people in America, we are met with police brutality and incarceration. The stories of Breonna Taylor, George Floyd, and Trayvon Martin, among innumerable others, show that the smallest offenses—from dating someone with a criminal record to selling bootleg cigarettes to walking through white neighborhoods—can lead to death at the hands of law enforcement and vigilantes. We are forced to conform to the rules of whiteness to keep our physical safety, job security, and other basic levels of comfort.

When I learned about the difference between race and ethnicity, it made me think more about our self-determination as Black people. African Americans are a people, not only connected by skin color but also by culture. Yet we do not have the right to control our own institutions, ways of life, and economic development.

In Cardi B's words, "Schools don't be teaching this shit to people."[52]

---

52 MaGee, "Fat Joe Talks Africa, Culture and Declares That 'Latinos Are Black.'"

CHAPTER 5

RAY

For where does one run to when he's already in the promised land?
—CLAUDE BROWN

My dad's sister says, "If you lived where you were not a novelty, you will never understand what that's like." My dad and his sister were the only Black children in their small Alaskan town. Other kids bounced pebbles off their hair and told their parents that they looked like little brown bears with no tails. My grandpa taught them to stand tall.

In 1959—the year Alaska became a US state and three years before my mother's birth—my dad's parents booked the whole family one-way tickets to the Last Frontier from St. Louis, Missouri. The same year they moved, the City of St. Louis bulldozed fifty-four blocks of primarily African American neighborhoods, destroyed 5,600 homes, and funneled those who lost their homes into inner-city housing projects far away from the new developments.[53] Grandpa Ray did

---

53   ArchCity Defenders et al., *Segregation in St. Louis: Dismantling the Divide* (St. Louis: Washington University in St. Louis, 2018).

not want his children raised in the systemic racism found in American inner cities.

Alaska had already been desegregated in 1945 through the Alaska Equal Rights Act, primarily due to the activism of a Tlingit, Alaska Native woman named Elizabeth Peratrovich.[54] *Color* and *Ebony* magazines published features on greater wages and job opportunities in Alaska compared to the Lower 48, declaring in 1958, "Alaska is a land of opportunity for hardworking pioneers with definite skills to offer."[55] After working ten years in the Air Force, Grandpa Ray had the opportunity to move his family north. He secured a job and housing with the Federal Aviation Administration at a small air traffic control tower in rural Alaska.

In Tanana and McGrath, the Stith family learned to do a lot of things on their own. There was one small trading post in town with just a few outrageously expensive groceries, so my grandma would order supplies like milk and flour from the bush planes that flew in according to schedule. Grandpa Ray took apart his daughter's dresses and sewed two more using the first as a pattern, taught himself to knit, and built the family a 6500-square-foot home.

Like most Alaskans, a lot of my dad's family's food came from the land. My grandpa grew up on a farm in Arkansas, and his knowledge about using a gun and producing food came in handy. They learned to run trap lines for mink and marten, tracked ptarmigan, hunted Dall sheep, and fished

---

54   Matthew Wills, "Alaska's Unique Civil Rights Struggle," *JSTOR Daily*, March 26, 2018.

55   Ian C. Hartman, "'Bonanza for Blacks?' Limits and Opportunities for African Americans in Southcentral Alaska," in *Imagining Anchorage: The Making of America's Northernmost Metropolis*, eds. James K. Barnett and Ian C. Hartman (Fairbanks: University of Alaska Press, 2018), 359-360.

all summer. By the time Grandpa Ray was elderly, I remember digging in his outdoor garden for carrots, cabbage, and collard greens.

This type of independence was what white leaders in cities like St. Louis aimed to prevent. Of the thousands of lynchings from the mid-1800s until the Civil Rights Movement, the majority were set in a rural backdrop of trees.[56] Black people who began to own land were swiftly punished. After the Civil War, white people murdered an estimated two to three Black people every week in large, public events to scare others into submission.[57] This pattern of white people's collective action against Black progress is coined "white rage."

Yet white rage is not about obvious violence; it primarily shows up in the courts, legislatures and government bureaucracies when Black people materially advance.[58] As Black Americans sought opportunity in cities north of the Mason Dixon, racist policies like Jim Crow, redlining, and urban renewal segregated Black people into inadequate public housing and underserved neighborhoods.[59] Rather than fund public services, Americans preferred to fund police. For example, 22 percent of the Anchorage Municipality's operating budget was designated for police in 2020. Health, as well as

---

56   Michael Starkley, "Wilderness, Race, and African Americans: An Environmental History from Slavery to Jim Crow" (master's thesis, University of California Berkeley, 2005), 37-40.

57   "Lynching in America," American Experience, PBS, accessed March 5, 2021.

58   Carol Anderson, *White Rage: The Unspoken Truth of Our Racial Divide* (New York: Bloomsbury Publishing, 2016), 4-5.

59   New York Law School Racial Justice Project, "Unshared Bounty: How Structural Racism Contributes to the Creation and Persistence of Food Deserts (with American Civil Liberties Union)," Racial Justice Project, Book 3 (2012), 6.

economic and community development line items equated to just 2 percent each, while the Equal Rights Commission received $775 total.[60]

In the post-Civil Rights era, lack of investment in our communities gnaws at our security and pride. Still today, Black communities are the most exposed to lead poisoning, airborne pollutants, built environments without greenery, and food deserts (the absence of adequate and nutritious grocery stores).[61,62] One often ignored consequence of systemic racism is that it severed many Black Americans' connection to the land.

My sister and I were city girls from Anchorage, only escaping to the rivers and mountains in the summer. When he took us fishing, snowshoeing, or camping, my dad's outrageous stories from childhood amazed us. He spent most of his childhood exploring the sub-Arctic pine forest, trying to catch Alaskan salmon with his bare hands, climbing to the tops of snow-laden roofs and sledding off them on sealskin parkas. My dad was in middle school when his family first moved to the big city, Anchorage. They stayed in the Wonder Park Motel for about three weeks upon arrival and, because it had a pool, the kids laughed and played all day like they were in Mexico. But Anchorage eventually became home and not a place for vacations.

By the time my dad and his sister came of age, it was the Ronald Reagan era. News from the Lower 48 described Black

---

60   2020 Proposed General Government Operating Budget (Anchorage: Municipality of Anchorage, 2020).

61   Ibid.

62   Jasmine Bell, "5 Things to Know About Communities of Color and Environmental Justice," *Race and Ethnicity* (blog), Center for American Progress, April 25, 2016.

people as criminals, crack babies, and welfare queens. When my dad's sister sought her first apartment in Anchorage, she was denied rental agreements. In fact, many Anchorage neighborhoods required homeowners to sign restrictive covenants pledging they would never sell to a non-white person—including the area I currently live in, Sand Lake and Spenard. The majority of real estate brokers refused to sell homes to Black and Alaska Native people outside Fairview and Mountainview, which were located in boggy lowlands without running water.[63]

Since Black and Indigenous people in my parents' generation were segregated to certain parts of Anchorage, white people in town had the unfair advantage of accumulating passive wealth over their lifetimes. The fact that only seven of America's 614 billionaires are Black and nearly 80 percent of millionaires are white is no coincidence, and our state and federal governments do little to redistribute that wealth.[64] Today, the wealth gap is worse between Black and white Americans than when my grandparents moved to Alaska. Many of my own peers who inherited wealth teased me about the racist stereotypes they still heard on television. But I knew my dad, and the more I learned about his story proved how much harder he had to work to support his family.

I'm proud to say my dad installed floors for a living; he worked with his hands. He would lift us into his Ford F150 pickup and drive us to some empty space, devoid of personality or decoration. He laid out the tiling, wood, or carpet, arranged it in order, and we helped him set it in place. After he

---

63 Hartman, "'Bonanza for Blacks?' Limits and Opportunities for African Americans in Southcentral Alaska," in *Imagining Anchorage: The Making of America's Northernmost Metropolis*.

64 Statistica, "Distribution of U.S. millionaires by race/ethnicity, as of 2013," accessed February 24, 2020.

finished, a loving couple would have a beautiful floor for their first dance; a new family got fresh carpets, ready to be stained with spills and messes. My dad brought scrap carpet home and duct-taped the swatches to our windows. I never had trouble sleeping through the midnight sun because of his homemade blinds. I still remember the smell of fresh carpet: wooly from the braided strands, sticky from the glue binding them.

Sometimes my dad picked me up from elementary school, and he always drew a lot of attention. I remember him standing in the middle of the cafeteria with four or five children climbing over him like a jungle gym. When he saw me, he clapped louder than any other human can: he cupped his big, calloused hands, clasped them together with a whooping sound, and you could hear it echo through the hallways. As he smiled, his two bottom teeth overlapped one another like they were hunched over in laughter. I remember having asked why he was so outgoing. He beamed, "I'm Black, and I'm proud!"

My dad's favorite color was lavender. I don't know why, but that seems relevant. For every part about himself that was beautiful, was also policed—no matter how far north we lived in the United States.

When my sister and I were still single digits in age, my parents used to take us sledding in a south Anchorage park called Oceanview Bluff. There was a network of parks nestled in a neighborhood of homes worth over three hundred thousand dollars, connected by wooded trails with the Alaska Railroad running through.

One summer we decided to take a stroll through the snowless park. My mom and dad led us hand in hand, cradling our little fingers on either side of them. A canopy of leaves ruffled above the four of us as we followed the path from the basketball court and parking lot to the grassy slope.

An older white couple led their yappy dog along the Alaska Railroad tracks that ran through the park.

Our walking path crossed directly over the tracks. Like we'd been taught in school, we looked left and right to make sure a train was not coming. Looking south over the tracks to the bluff park, a line of mansions and a slope covered in birches and pines led to shimmering mud flats, giving way to the wide sparkling ocean. A breeze blew our hair around our faces, and the only sound was the soft whistle of wind.

Our parents gave the okay to cross and, just as soon as we did, a white officer approached us.

"I just remember being approached by the person telling us that we needed to get off the track," my mom recalled. "And the reason I remember wondering why he approached us is because the other couple literally walked down the track—you could see that it was their purpose—and we were only crossing an established path."

Six-foot-two and darker-skinned than his father, my dad must have always been an object of scrutiny in his lifelong home. He went to jail multiple times, though that phase of his life seemed to have finished for most of my childhood. It is true he broke laws and was not perfect. But every single human has done bad things, and Black people receive the swiftest punishment with the least compassion.

Mass incarceration has been a primary tool of oppression since the Civil Rights era began; in the late 1960s and 1970s, Black and Native Alaskans received between 277 and 683 percent longer sentences than white offenders for the same crimes.[65] With more than two million prisoners, the

<hr />

65   Hartman, "'Bonanza for Blacks?' Limits and Opportunities for African Americans in Southcentral Alaska," in *Imagining Anchorage: The Making of America's Northernmost Metropolis.*

United States incarcerates more people than China, Russia, and every other country in the world.[66] Prisons serve to disappear the systemic problems white policymakers have so far refused to solve.[67]

I don't know what went through my dad's head as he took his life at fifty years old, surrounded by police and the Anchorage SWAT team aiming guns at him. I used to speculate that he couldn't bear the reality of going back to prison, having his freedom stripped away, and losing years with his children. But it is also possible that police were prepared to kill him. The choice he made in those hopeless, frightened moments allowed him some agency to determine his future.

When my dad's family moved to Alaska, they did it by taking up space in white institutions. The closer non-white people can get to whiteness through mannerisms of speaking, presentation, credentials, and physical proximity, the easier navigating western society can be.[68] But along the way, white rage demands us to give up our own traditions, culture, and sense of place.

I often feel like a piece of me is missing. I wonder what I would be like had I known my dad longer or had I grown up around more Black people. Learning more about my family's and America's history helped me find peace with our story. His memory continues to drive my passion for more just policies and decision-making.

---

66   Statistica Research Department, "Countries with the Largest Number of Prisoners, as of June 2020," Statistica, December 1, 2020.

67   Angela Y. Davis, *Are Prisons Obsolete?* (New York: Seven Stories Press, 2003), 16.

68   Edmund Ruge, "Black Self-determination Drawn From Our Roots," *Peripheries Journal* no. 5 (2020).

CHAPTER 6

KENAI

———

[I]f we allow the Arctic to melt, we lose more than the
planet that has nurtured us for all of human history.
We lose the wisdom required for us to sustain it.

— SHEILA WATT-CLOUTIER

I grew up around the water because my dad was an avid
fisherman. At his funeral his best friends said, "He could
catch a fish out of a bucket." He was the type to wake
the family up at 3 a.m. to drive to the fishing hole so
we could be on the beach for the 6 a.m. salmon run. My
dad cleaned and filleted the fish by hand, then froze the
majority of our catch for the family's meals through the
winter and spring.

As a young adult, those cherished memories were one
reason why I chose to study environmental science and policy.
Historically, Black Americans relied on hunting and fishing
to supplement their food. The skill was especially useful
when low wages did not match the high costs of food during
Jim Crow and, before that, when people who claimed them

as property provided insufficient rations.[69] But the pinnacle environmental texts of the twentieth century completely excluded Black people. In a college course about environmental history in North America, I learned that the likes of John Muir believed wilderness should be untouched by humans, preserved for the exhilaration and enjoyment of the upper class when they felt like leaving the city.

A lot of us subconsciously believe in manifest destiny: that the US was destined to be its current size, and that the American continent was unaltered by people before the arrival of white explorers.[70] Yet in order to delineate wilderness spaces, Indigenous peoples were forcibly relocated, arrested when found fishing or hunting in places they always had, and killed to create National Parks.[71] Also, Jim Crow laws outlawed Black Americans from hunting and fishing in order to limit their independent travel and survival.[72] Black peoples' and Indigenous peoples' exclusion from environmental decision-making has always been a way to control their resources. Today, federal and state governments continue to enforce the idea that nature must be separated from humans and their economies.

You see, there are multiple types of economies. In a capitalist economy, private entities sell goods and services for

---

69 Michael Starkley, "Wilderness, Race, and African Americans: An Environmental History from Slavery to Jim Crow" (master's thesis, University of California Berkeley, 2005), 37-40.

70 Roxanne Dunbar-Ortiz, "Excerpt: An Indigenous Peoples' History of the United States," Beacon Press, accessed April 16, 2021.

71 Mark David Spence, *Dispossessing the Wilderness: Indian Removal and the Making of the National Parks* (Oxford: Oxford University Press, 2000), 55-70.

72 Ibid.

profit. In a socialist economy, the government owns production and makes goods and services accessible to the public. And in a subsistence economy, people rely on the land and water to provide goods and services directly to one another.

In Alaska, 95 percent of rural Alaskan households participate in subsistence fishing.[73] Including mammals, shellfish, birds, eggs, and fish, Alaskans harvest about 33.6 million pounds each year. I was so little when I started fishing that my first word was 'ish.

"We went dip netting on the Kenai River with some friends," my mom told me. "We took our haul of fish back to their cabin and laid the fish out on the lawn side by side to count how many fish there were."

I sat on the grass and ogled at the long line of king salmon. The fish had hooked snouts and freckled backs. The reds from the Kenai River were about as long as I was tall: just under three feet. When I brushed my tiny fingers from snout to tail, the skin felt slimy and smooth. In the other direction, my fingernails caught on the thin, translucent scales.

"Ish!" I shouted. My parents ran over, hugged me, and took turns posing for pictures with me and the fresh catch.

By my first birthday, my family had already taken me fly fishing on the Russian River and dip netting in the Kenai River, the traditional homelands of Ahtna and Dena'ina people. The name Kenai comes from the Kenaitze Indian Tribe: a sovereign, independent Dena'ina nation. Catching and sharing fish among the tribe is the way they always lived. Therefore, federal laws acknowledge that the Kenaitze's right to fish for subsistence is crucial to their

---

73 Division of Subsistence, *Subsistence in Alaska: A Year 2017 Update* (Anchorage: Alaska Department of Fish & Game, 2018).

self-determination—their ability to freely pursue their economic, social, and cultural development.[74]

Yet, back in the 1980s, the State of Alaska deliberately misinterpreted the Alaska National Interest Lands Conservation Act (ANILCA) to deny special privileges to subsistence users on the Kenai. The state gave commercial and sports fishermen just as much access to the fisheries, if not more, and the vast influx of Anchorage residents created a cash economy on the Kenai Peninsula. Rather than allowing their right to fish for the community, the state enforced a socioeconomic shift among Dena'ina.[75]

When I participated in Kenai dipnet fishing at the height of king salmon season as a toddler, thousands of fishermen lined the river's shallow banks. Everyone strapped up in their chest waders, which essentially looked like overall-style footy pajamas made of rubber and neoprene. The adults packed layers of shirts, jackets and long underwear underneath their rubber suits.

On the riverbank, fishers sweated under all the gear weighing them down. With dry-suit footies stuffed into porous wading shoes, they took heavy, controlled steps into the eighty-two-mile-long channel. But as soon as they stepped into the racing river, the cold, dense water rushed through the space between their toes and boots. It sucked the air from inside their waders and flattened the clothing layers against their skin.

My dad taught me the fight with the fish was the most exciting part: the bigger the fight, the bigger the fish, and the taller fish tales he could tell. The fishers dangled five-foot-wide

---

74 Kenaitze Indian Tribe v. State of Alaska, 860 F.2d 312 (1988).

75 Ibid.

nets in front of twenty-foot-long wooden and metal poles. The goal was to stick their nets as far into the river as possible; as the salmon swam with the current down the middle of the channel, they swam directly into the nets and jerked wildly. Fishers quickly rotated the poles against the current until their hoops touched the river's sandy bottom and triumphantly dragged their catch backward to shore. They packed their coolers to the brim, taking twenty-five fresh salmon apiece.

It's hard to believe that this huge event, which certainly affected the Kenaitze's way of life, barely makes a dent in Alaska's fish populations. The total subsistence catch for Alaska represents only 0.9 percent of the tonnage of fish caught in the state, compared to 98.6 percent, or nearly 3.8 billion pounds of fish, that are caught commercially.[76] That magnitude of resource extraction does make a dent. With current commercial activity around the world, nearly all seafood stocks could face 90 percent depletion by 2050.[77]

When I volunteered to take notes at the 2017 Yukon River Inter-Tribal Watershed Council Summit, far north of where I grew up, chiefs and village representatives repeatedly articulated that commercial fishing reduces salmon runs. By law, the state must preference subsistence use over commercial fisheries. According to the Alaska Department of Fish and Game, the state has eighty-one state advisory committees for locals to make recommendations on management of Alaska's fish and wildlife.[78] But Indigenous leaders' repeated testimonies have not resulted in systemic change to fisheries management.

---

76 Division of Subsistence, *Subsistence in Alaska*.

77 Boris Worm et al., "Impacts of Biodiversity Loss on Ocean Ecosystem Services," *Science* 314 no. 5800 (2006): 787-790.

78 Alaska Department of Fish and Game, "Regulations," accessed February 28, 2021.

One note I'd taken said, "We have advisory committees in the village, but no one is required to listen to us."

The main way commercial fishing rights are regulated in Alaska is individual transferable quotas (ITQ). Fishers with ITQs can catch certain amounts of fish for commercial sale or sell their quotas to other fishers. The problem with the ITQ system is that people with more wealth can afford to catch more fish. Over time, the right to fish increasingly concentrated in the relatively more cash-wealthy hands of white men, while Indigenous fishers and women have been squeezed out of fisheries.[79]

Modern-day stereotypes reinforce ideas that white people are the main leaders in environmentalism, creating "landscapes of exclusion."[80] In the case of ITQs in Alaska, it was primarily white scientists who set the total catch limits for Alaska, primarily white people with masters' degrees who led the management of ITQs and now, disproportionately white people owning quotas. In Alaska and other Arctic fisheries, resources that were always available for subsistence are now owned by the highest bidder.

The fact of the matter is that Indigenous peoples have touched and shaped this landscape for centuries upon centuries. There are very many different Indigenous peoples with distinct cultures and traditions—in Alaska alone there are Iñupiaq Yupik, Unangax̂ (Aleut), Eyak, Tlingit, Haida, Tsimshian, and a number of Northern Dene (Athabaskan) peoples—but some similarities connect them. Many

79 Oran R. Young et al., "Moving beyond panaceas in fisheries governance." *Proceedings of the National Academy of Sciences* 115, no. 37: 2018.

80 Carolyn Finney, *Black Faces, White Spaces: Reimagining the Relationship of African Americans to the Great Outdoors* (Chapel Hill: The University of North Carolina Press, 2014), 10.

Indigenous communities use the entire body of animals they catch not only for food, but for clothing, shelter, tools, toys and means of transport. The catch supports not only the hunter or fisher's household, but multiple families in the community. After thousands of years of providing from the land, intergenerational knowledge about the environment guides subsistence.

As only the second generation to live in Alaska, I don't have that deep knowledge about subsistence and environmental stewardship. I and many others before me argue that Alaska Native peoples should have more control over fisheries and other natural resources and should receive adequate funding to do so. After all, Alaska only boasts such rich bounties of fish and wildlife because of the Alaskans who stewarded the land for millennia.[81]

In the origin stories of many Alaska Native peoples, animals could talk and taught humans lessons about life.[82] Many times I heard the story of when humans first arrived in Alaska. The animals remarked that humans had no fur, sharp teeth nor claws to protect them. *How will they survive?* the animals wondered. To help the humans, the animals offered their bodies for food and clothing. The sacrifice was a precious one, so humans learned to respect them. They knew the land was plentiful, but never took more from it than they needed.

---

81 Native Peoples Action, "An Indigenous Vision for Our Collective Future: Becoming Earth's Stewards Again," *Nonprofit Quarterly* (Fall 2020).

82 Peter Kalifornsky and Katherine McNamara, *From the First Beginning, When the Animals Were Talking: On the Writing and Thought of Peter Kalifornsky*, Apple Books, accessed February 20, 2021.

To say the animals used to talk implies they don't any-more. But the land, plants, and animals still provide lessons. The heart of the matter is that humans very rarely listen.[83]

Unlike my friends in urban and suburban parts of the United States, I learned to be intimately aware that food came from living creatures. Salmon have impressive life cycles. After hatching in Alaskan rivers, salmon fry grow without parents, find their way to the ocean by instinct, survive among much larger predators for six years—some migrating over two thousand miles—to finally return home to Alaska for spawning. To eat salmon meant to take their lives from them, and we should respect that sacrifice.

My dad kept a short wooden bat strapped to his hip. It was birch color and stained dark with use. When he landed a fish, he passed me the bat, laid down his pole or net, threaded his finger through its gills with one hand and gripped the tail with the other.

"Will it hurt him?" I asked. The salmon wriggled back and forth under his grip.

"Whack hard, right there on the top of its head," my dad reassured me. "Quick, so it doesn't feel much pain."

To help me out, he counted. One... two... and on three, I quickly struck the fish on the top of the head. Then my dad strung a rope through its gills, anchored the rope to the shore so the fish's body floated in the river, and waded back into the water. By the time I was five, one of my most frequent roles was Fish Killer.

83 Deenaalee Hodgdon and Haliehana Stepetin, "Xilegg I. Mapping: Accessing Indigenous Belonging to Place w/ Haliehana Stepetin," November 30, 2020, in *On The Land: Stories from the People, Stories from the Land*, produced by Deenaalee Hodgdon, podcast, MP3 audio, 24:00-40:00.

By six years old, I had my own pair of hip waders. With river water rushing past my legs, I watched my three-year-old sister on the shore. She was so small that she couldn't fish; she would bring Tupperware to the river and chase salmon fry. I waded down the river while squinting through the water, searching for full-grown fish in my green waders and my dad's polarized glasses. On my ninth birthday, he gave me a custom fishing rod with the words engraved, "Come to mama, fishy" (my own inspirational words).

"Another time we went dip netting on the Kenai, do you remember the lady who cut out a salmon heart, gathered a bunch of kids and showed it to us?" I asked my mom. She's always been a petite lady, just shy of five feet tall. Now the part in her hair showcases a stylish, natural gray streak. Even when I was little, her hair was never longer than her chin.

"I definitely remember the event," she replied.

I remember the gray, rocky Kenai River shore with smooth flat stones that seemed to stretch for miles. The river was cold and windy, but the fishers still fished, so we splashed around the beach in rain hats, boots, and jackets. There was movement and excitement regardless of dreary weather.

A woman had caught my attention as she lugged a fish up the beach and away from the water. She waved her arms to beckon us over.

"I don't remember who the woman was though," my mom said.

A group of kids under twelve years old gathered around the lady. She knelt to the ground with a cutting board in front of her. A filet knife lay beside it, sharp and long. She held the fish with one hand looped through its gills and the other around its tail. She placed the fish on the cutting board; its silver scales gleamed under cloudy skies. Opening the belly, she pulled out two sacks clustering hundreds of red liquid eggs.

"A female," she said. Next, she laid a brown-red triangle on the cutting board (the liver) and grabbed the other guts with her hand to slosh them in a bucket.

"This is the heart." She reached into the area near the salmon's head and cut out a brownish-red pyramid the size of a bonbon. A thin, yellowish vascular tube donned one end. She gingerly passed the heart to her palm and stretched out her hand for our big eyes to feast on. The organ squeezed up, then relaxed.

"Oh my gosh!" one of us yelled. Our curious eyes locked on the organ, waiting.

Then it beat again.

"Ahhh!" We all giggled and squealed.

"A salmon's heart continues beating for a few minutes after it dies," she told us, passing the heart from the palm of each child to the next. I felt in my hands that the salmon's heartbeat was like ours. Energy still coursed through it for those few moments; muscles spasmed without central command.

Long after sixth grade, when my dad passed away, our cherished memories on the water stayed core to my identity. On the ocean, at a river or a stream, I recall our summers fishing together. Humans need this personal, community-based kind of relationship with food to remind ourselves of the importance and value of the environment.

The way that commercial fisheries are set up does not support a relationship with fish. The vast majority of our wild Alaskan salmon are exported to other parts of the country and the world; the carbon emissions required to ship it contribute to climate change; the fins, scales, and heads are discarded, never to be used; and profits ultimately fall into hands of corporate entities, rather than the people who stewarded the land for generations. Capitalist extraction takes the fundamentally Christian view that humans "possess" land and resources, and that the riches gotten from it shall be passed down from father to son.[84] This worldview leads to unsustainable, world-changing consumption, affecting everything from Alaskan fisheries to the Amazon rainforest.

But wildlife managers and many people who claim to be environmentalists simply don't know how to live more sustainably. The economic systems we rely upon are so far removed from the land. Meanwhile, the people who do know about the environment are deeply excluded from systems of power and decision-making. It is my firm belief that the solutions to a biodiverse, climate-balanced Earth will come from strengthening Indigenous peoples' control over their own lands and resources.

---

84 OpenBible.info, "100 Bible Verses about Buying Land," accessed February 28, 2021.

CHAPTER 7

TROPENATT

So we are left with a stark choice: Allow climate disruption to change everything about our world or change pretty much everything about our economy to avoid that fate. But we need to be very clear: Because of our decades of collective denial, no gradual, incremental options are now available to us.

—NAOMI KLEIN

Before Norway, I had attended school in Durham, North Carolina for the prior four years. The climate was exciting for the first few weeks I was a freshman. During the day I brought my towel and highlighters to the lawn, studied my assigned readings, and sunbathed in 105-degree heat. I remember sitting on the bench outside my dorm at 10 p.m., when the air was still humid and the sky pitch black. I marveled at the chorus of cicadas, grasshoppers, and creatures filling the night. I had never experienced darkness and heat at the same time; in Alaska, the sun scarcely set during our few months of summer.

I could only remember one or two times Anchorage had reached eighty degrees. Since our freshman dorm didn't have air conditioning, my sweet, wonderful roommate from Georgia taught me how to set up a fan in our window. We spent many nights splayed on our separate bunks, unable to get up or do anything except wallow in our pools of sweat. Once I nearly passed out from overheating inside the butterfly greenhouse on campus. I was *not* raised to withstand heat.

When I came to Norway, I expected cold. I wanted to be part of the people who—in the face of climate change—fought to preserve the cold. The summer I arrived, though, was one of the hottest ever recorded. Not only in Tromsø, not only in Norway, but during 2018, the temperature in the high Arctic was four degrees hotter than the long-term 1958–2002 average.[85] Climate change was affecting the Arctic much faster than the rest of the world.

Hot days were an exasperating reminder I couldn't possibly work hard enough to affect Arctic environmental policies. On the early morning of July 31, 2018, I panted down the hill to the Secretariat, stopped at the bathroom to pat moisture from my face, then buzzed my ID card to let myself into the office.

"Good morning," I said, peeking into one of the hall offices.

"Beautiful day, isn't it?" My colleague smiled back. Large windows filled half the wall in her modern office, so I could see the Fram Centre *lysgården* behind her.

"I suppose," I frowned. "It's a scorcher. I didn't expect summer to be like this." The night before, my room had turned into a sauna. Like many Arctic homes, my *kollektiv* was sturdily insulated for Arctic winter and not equipped with air conditioning. The sun hadn't set the night before, and the heat from the previous day just seemed to accumulate.

---

85   "Arctic +80 North Temperature," Danish Meteorological Institute, accessed February 25, 2021.

"No, it's very unusual," she responded with some sadness.

She motioned me over to look at the news on her computer screen: "Ekstraordinært vær i nord: 30 grader og tropenatt" sprawled across the screen. *Extraordinary weather in the north: 30 degrees and tropical night.*[86]

"This was the first ever *tropenatt*, tropical night, recorded in Tromsø," she said.

"Tropical night?" I questioned.

"Det betyr at temperaturen ikke bikker under 20 grader i løpet av natta," she read. "The temperature never dropped below 20 degrees last night."

That's 68 degrees Fahrenheit—20 degrees higher than the average nighttime temperature in Tromsø from 1985–2015.[87]

"It's already 30 degrees today?" I asked, still very unsure about Celsius.

"In Troms, it's 32.7 today," she said.

I typed in the conversion on my phone: 90.9 degrees Fahrenheit.

Though this is drastic for an Arctic summer, climate change is most noticeable during polar night in the far North, when the sun dips below the Arctic horizon for two months. Tromsø's winters are seventeen days shorter than they used to be, and long-term winter temperatures in some Arctic places are up to 8 degrees Celsius above normal.[88,89] On average,

86 Vilde Kristine Malmo, "Ekstraordinært vær i nord: 30 grader og tropenatt," NRK/NTB, July 17, 2018.

87 CustomWeather, "Climate & Weather Averages in Tromsø, Norway," Time and Date AS, accessed October 5, 2020.

88 Thomas Nilsen, "The Tromsø-winter now 17 days shorter than 30 years ago," *The Barents' Observer*, January 8, 2020.

89 "Arctic +80 North Temperature," Danish Meteorological Institute, accessed February 24, 2021.

Anchorage's annual temperature increased more than 2.5 degrees Celsius since my dad was born in 1959.[90]

To put that in perspective, 174 countries and the European Union agreed to limit carbon emissions under the Paris Climate Accord so the world's average annual temperature would not increase more than 2 degrees Celsius from pre-industrial levels.[91] But our globe has already heated up 1.3 degrees Celsius. Without drastic action, the Earth could *easily* warm 3 or 4 degrees in the next eighty years.

Think about how drastically the Earth will change in our lifetimes. During the last Ice Age, the earth was only 6 degrees Celsius colder, on average, than in pre-industrial times.[92]

Today's weather undoubtedly left me conflicted. From the office window, the sky shone a vibrant blue and fluffy white clouds circulated sparsely around. The ocean just beyond the seaside building sparkled with sunlight. The grass on the lawn, trees on the mountainside, and even weeds in the concrete seemed leafy and ultra-green. It was a gorgeous, tropical day. All I really wanted to do was lie outside and soak it up.

There is one thing Alaskans and Norwegians have in common: we never want to waste a sunny day, because we never know when we'll see another one. I greeted the three or four other people in the office—still a third of our usual staff—and sat down to work. After only a couple hours at the

---

90 Municipality of Anchorage, *Climate Action Plan* (Anchorage: Municipality of Anchorage, 2019).

91 Melissa Denchak, "Paris Climate Agreement: Everything You Need to Know," National Resource Defense Council, January 15, 2021.

92 Will Dunham, "Scientists have figured out just how cold the last Ice Age was. Here's why it matters, "*Global Agenda* (blog), World Economic Forum, September 1, 2020.

desk, the director walked around and informed everyone that the office would be closed for the rest of the day.

"It is very nice today, so please go outside," she told us authoritatively. "Your job today is to enjoy the weather."

I didn't have to be told twice. I packed up my things, scurried back up the hill to my house, and changed from my office wear into shorts and hiking boots. By 1:30 p.m., I was ready to board a bus that would take me straight to the outskirts of Tromsø mainland. This would be the first time I tackled Tromsø buses alone.

Anna had told me not to stand closer than a meter from other people waiting at the bus stop. I fumbled with the Tromsø Ruter app alone on the street corner. While waiting for the bus to rumble down the hill, I silently soaked in my surroundings. There was a gaudy white house with pink-, green-, and yellow-painted window frames across the street from the bus stop. In black English letters the owner had painted "It's Never Too Late to Be a Rock Star" across the front.

When the bus pulled up, I flashed the app's active ticket at the driver. The doors closed behind me and immediately entrapped me in the heat of a car that's been baking in a parking lot all day.

You must not sit next to or talk to anyone on the bus, I remembered. Ten or so people spaced themselves at least two rows apart. I steadied myself on the warm yellow bars as the bus pulled off, then took a window seat by myself.

I guzzled from my water bottle as houses passed by. Most houses in Tromsø seemed similar in size to my *kollektiv.* They looked like suburban homes, but the population density of any given street would make you think there were apartment buildings all over. While America's suburbs require families to fuel large homes and cars to commute, Europe's cities allow populations to produce much fewer carbon emissions with buses, trains, and more efficient living spaces. In fact, simply living in Norway reduced the size of my carbon footprint.

In the Nordics, urban planning is usually centered around people's mobility, livability, and sustainability.[93] Gravity pushed my back against the bus seat as we drove over Tromsøbrua, the large bridge that connects Tromsøya to mainland Tromsø. It arcs over the sea at thirty-six meters (one hundred twenty-five feet tall). Two narrow lanes hugged each other across the bridge but, instead of a shoulder on each side, a fenced-off walkway and bike lane straddled either edge. I rode in a car maybe a dozen times while I was in the country; the rest was walking and public transport.

I couldn't tell if the heat under my collar was from the *tropenatt*, or the way I envied Norwegians. In the United States, 40 percent of bridges need to be replaced or repaired.[94] But the infrastructure problem is even more pronounced in Alaska, where the majority of towns are only accessible by plane or boat. In thirty unserved villages across the state, more than 3,300 Alaskans live without flush toilets and running water.[95] Alaska's governor also slashed funding to the Marine Highway System in 2018 and, in the same year, cut 40 percent of the University of Alaska's budget.[96],[97] Ultimately,

---

93 Maddy Savage, "What the Nordic nations can teach us about liveable cities," *Worklife* (blog), BBC, November 12, 2019.

94 American Road and Transportation Builders Association, "Bridge Report," last updated March 11, 2021.

95 Division of Water, "Alaska Water and Sewer Challenge (AWSC)," Department of Environmental Conservation, accessed March 24, 2021.

96 Chia-Yi Hou, "Alaska Governor Cuts $130 Million for University of Alaska System," *The Scientist*, July 1, 2019.

97 James Brooks, "Ferries on the chopping block and cuts to Pioneer Homes: A rundown of how Gov. Dunleavy's budget cuts would affect Alaskans," *Anchorage Daily News*, February 13, 2019.

the conservative State of Alaska does not make enough money from taxes to fund adequate public services—whether they be infrastructure, health, or education.

In Norway, no one has to worry about those risks. Thanks to a generous oil revenue fund and progressively higher taxes for wealthy citizens, every Norwegian has guaranteed housing, universal health care, and nearly free education. They even forgive student loans for youth who settle in the Arctic. While Norway's government redistributes wealth, Alaska's government skims a percentage from oil revenues for minimal public services.[98]

I pressed my forehead against the scalding window and shielded my eyes to look over the side of the bridge. Long metal poles acted like a rib cage around the bridge, shielding pedestrians and bikers from its edge. I could imagine how scary it would be to take the twenty-minute walk up and across on a windy day. It's still not as scary as living under the whim of corporations.

In America and especially Alaska, we are taught that taxes are bad and the government can't be trusted with our money. We trust for-profit companies to provide services like healthcare and insurance, transportation, and private education instead. Yet, unlike governments, corporations have no accountability to us. While living in Norway, it became clear that America's preference toward under-regulated, under-taxed capitalism inhibits equity. Corporate influence on government has slashed the top one percent's minimum tax rates in half in the last sixty years; raising the top one percent's effective tax rate by just 25 percentage points would still leave them with an average annual

---

98 Dermot Cole, "How Norway and Alaska took different paths when it came to investing windfalls from oil development," *ArcticToday*, March 10, 2018.

after-tax income of over one million dollars and generate eight trillion for the rest of us.[99,100]

I shut my eyes and attempted to block out these thoughts, to let the sun shine on my face. *Remember, Michaela,* I told myself, *you're supposed to be relaxing.*

At each stop, a mechanical voice cut through the silent heat of the bus. I mouthed the words, though the pronunciation didn't match what I read on the screen listing upcoming stops. I learned not to trust my pronunciation of written Norwegian. Some stops looked similar to English (*Midnattsolvegen* was Midnight Sun Street) but sounded very different. "Toe-mas yoord-nes." *Tomasjordnes.* "Owstime noord." *Austheim nord.* The ride took about twenty minutes total until I arrived at Kroken: "Krook-en." I pulled the yellow cord by my head, deboarded the bus, and followed a map on the Norwegian hiking association app up to the trailhead.

Many hikers before me had carved a dirt path into the hill. The hillside was made up of a lot of boulders overgrown with lichen, crowberry bushes and tiny green shrubs. Shaggy fungi and red mushrooms with white freckles peeked out between the flora-covered mounds. Skinny birch trees grew upward like vines without a fence to hold onto; they curled and twisted up to the sun because the boulders constantly pushed their roots downhill. To my left, the sound of a babbling stream tickled my ears. The landscape was whimsical and the brightest green I could imagine.

All that oxygen, the fresh smells of green leaves and fungi, and the movement in my limbs was something I missed. Although North Carolina is also known for some of its parks,

---

99 "Fact Sheet: Taxing Wealthy Americans," Americans for Tax Fairness, 2014.

100 Michael Linden, "What could the US afford if it raised billionaires' taxes? We do the math," *The Guardian*, December 13, 2019.

I hadn't had time to hike there. Instead, I spent all-nighters writing twenty-thousand-word papers, power-walked from one class to the next, and booked the rest of my time with on-campus jobs and student leadership positions—all so, one day, I would reap the benefits of a dream job.

For the first few minutes, I powered up the hiking trail. Hiking in the North is usually accompanied by a forgiving breeze that wicks sweat from my skin, but the ninety-degree heat had no mercy on me. I was always pushing myself toward some goal—fighting climate change, securing my dream job, summiting this mountain.

In the United States, Americans race toward economic security as if there's a mountain to summit. From the moment we enter school, we're taught the American dream: if I hustle hard enough, brave through the heat and uphill climb, one day I might achieve wealth and security. But, when the hike starts, they forget to mention that some of us will start at the bottom of the hill, some will start very near the top, some will be dropped off at the bus stop and have to find the trail to begin with. Those who start with economic security, who were born at the top of the mountain, only have to keep from sliding down.

In reality, economic inequality is now at its highest, and upward mobility from our parents' tax brackets is nearly impossible. In the history of the United States, the government has made no successful redress to close the economic gap caused by legally enforced enslavement, segregation, historic nor contemporary discrimination.[101] Without redistribution of wealth led by government policies, America's racial wealth gap will likely continue for another 450 years.

---

101 William A. Darity and A. Kirsten Mullen, *From Here to Equality: Reparations for Black Americans in the Twenty-First Century* (Chapel Hill: The University of North Carolina Press, 2020), 1-6.

Redistribution of wealth would also be better for the environment. Access to capital is the greatest determinant of each person's carbon footprint: the richest 10 percent of the world's population (about 630 million people) were responsible for 52 percent of carbon emissions from 1990 to 2015. Emissions continued to grow over that period, and the top 5 percent alone contributed one-third of the growth.[102] The rate at which very wealthy people consume resources is not sustainable, and neither is perpetual economic growth.

The thing is, our need to continue moving at all levels of society is because growth-oriented capitalism requires constant resource extraction and consumption at concentrated levels year-round. Not only does the nonstop nature of our economy stress our psyches, but it stresses the environment.

Many of the inches-tall baby birches springing from the forest floor could only grow there because of the warming climate. I hiked uphill about thirty minutes, sweat drenching my clothes, before I decided the hike wasn't worth it. All of us, including me, need rest. Everything around me was too beautiful to be hot and miserable.

A small offshoot from the trail beckoned me toward the stream. I climbed around large, round boulders dotted with stubbly yellow-green lichens, flat and smooth white lichen, flaky orange lichen (can you tell how much I love lichens…) and fuzzy black moss to get to the water. The boulders dammed up the water every so often, forming pools that gently flowed downhill, bubbled up, and made a powerful sound cascading over boulders. I could see straight through the pool to gray, orange, white and black pebbles nestled between them.

---

102 Tim Gore, "Confronting Carbon Inequality: Putting Climate Justice at the Heart of the COVID-19 Recovery," Oxfam Media Briefing, September 21, 2020.

On either side of the stream, the land gently sloped toward and blocked it from view. The entire hillside was made of round humps covered in the greenest of green mosses, succulent-soft berry bushes, and fanned ferns. Zoom out from the small details, and the trees stole the scene. Imagine the flimsiest, most twisted looking birches less than ten feet tall, coiling and craning for the bright afternoon sun.

I sprawled out on a flat rock on the edge of the stream, closed my eyes, and tried to relax. I took a deep breath in and let the babbling brook fill my ears. On the exhale, I felt the sun's warmth freckle my cheeks.

While a hot day was nice every once in a while, I hoped I wouldn't ever see a time when drizzly, cool Arctic summers would be gone; when I couldn't recognize the places I grew up in. I knew, unfortunately, that the rate our world was addressing climate change would probably ring the day in sooner rather than later.

3

FALL

CHAPTER 8

BESTEVENN

———

*We have to talk about liberating minds
as well as liberating society.*

—ANGELA Y. DAVIS

As the midnight sun's heat morphed into shorter fall days, Anna and Nora took me under their Norwegian wings. We frequented Prestvannet, a lake within walking distance of our *kollektiv*. At the height of gull season, we decided to hike around the lake to feed ducks. We ended up running from twenty-pound raucous seagulls dive-bombing toward the bread bags in our arms. The three of us lifted our hoods and sprinted far into the distance. On this side of the lake, a group of ducks waddled near an empty bench. Their little brown bottoms wiggled back and forth while they quacked at our breadcrumbs. In their midst, a seagull crouched on the ground, waddled its white behind, and tweeted its best impression of a quack.

I felt like that seagull a lot—the odd one out trying hard to fit in, often embarrassing myself even if just for a few measly crumbs.

"How do you make friends in Norway?" I asked when we walked back to the *kollektiv*. I had met a lot of people at Riddu Riđđu, but friends like Ture-Biehtar were spread out over Norway, Finland, Sweden, and Russia. Marja and I followed up on plans to hang out in Tromsø, but she left the country to study abroad in the end of August. "I read you're supposed to join events and organized activities, so that's why I've been volunteering at festivals. But if you have any advice…"

"Herregud," Anna exclaimed. *Oh my God.* She threw her hands in the air. "You're asking *me* about making friends?"

Nora shook her head. "Friends are hard."

It turns out that I was overachieving when counting new friends. Gaining Anna and Nora in only two months was unheard of. The two of them had just started new jobs: Nora as a construction guard along Tromsøbrua, Anna teaching toddlers at a local *kindergarten*. (Confusingly, kindergarten is the Norwegian word for "preschools.") Other than their colleagues, they hadn't met anyone new. Nora told me that when her mom moved to her dad's hometown, she did not make a new friend for six years.

I was lucky. Anna decided she loved me the first day we met in July. Whenever she talked about me to Nora when I wasn't around, she called me her *bestevenn*, best friend. But she was too shy to tell me that herself, at first.

In general, Norwegians are very reserved. New people can feel scary, and it is more comfortable for Norwegians to assess someone from afar. For example, I learned it's not allowed to invite a friend from one group to join activities with friends from another group. Making new friends was difficult primarily because of Norwegian social rules.

Toward the end of September, I wrote this extended list of rules:

- You must not talk to strangers in Norway.
- You must not acknowledge acquaintances in public.
- You must not bring friends from one social group to an event hosted by a separate group.
- You must always wear proper outdoor gear.
- You must never walk in the street. Only cross the street at proper crosswalks and when there is a walking sign.

I learned the rules bit by bit. When I made too much noise or walked out of place on the street, other pedestrians locked eyes with me and glared. When I acted out of place among friends, they corrected or side-eyed me. I crossed Anna and Nora walking up and down the hill to our house sometimes. When I called out and waved from a distance the first time, they hid their faces in their hoods and ignored me.

Another time I was in the grocery store searching for hot chocolate for our movie night and couldn't find the right brand. I FaceTimed Anna to ask what kind she wanted.

She answered the phone: "Ha? Where are you?"

"I'm in the grocery store," I said.

"What! Don't FaceTime in the grocery store. Norwegians don't do that." She hung up.

All those rules made it hard to be social in general. Everyone I talked to would like to make friends more easily, but they worried how others would perceive them. Norwegians impose these rules on themselves more than anyone else: Nora and Anna were so nervous to talk to other people because they were always afraid of making themselves outcasts.

"You're very open," Nora commented.

She told me later how she struggled with overthinking social situations. She believed that the worst kind of people were people who didn't think about others before spewing out words. "Cool people"—the best kind of people—were usually not the popular ones. Cool people were kind and self-assured; they didn't have to worry about what other people thought of them, but always knew how to treat other people right. She thought I was like that: completely carefree and self-assured.

In my view, the best kind of people were those who had *been through* something. Resilience was the highest virtue. It doesn't matter to me how people get up, but that they keep going. Though we all want to be liked, I'd never been able to please everyone.

"You can talk to strangers because you're American," Anna said. "If you start talking to people in English, they'll lo-ove it."

"But not us," Nora confirmed.

The strict social rules I noticed are related to a phenomenon called the Laws of Jante, a set of cultural rules historically observed Scandinavia.[103] They go something like, "Don't think you are better than we are; don't think you know more than we do; don't think you can teach us anything." I got the impression that Norwegians were not particularly fond of these laws. Many would say that these rules are waning, young people have grown out of them, and they are oversimplified to begin with. I think this is true. In some ways, these rules are no different than any other culture's in the way they enforce social norms and customs.

Still, as an American, reading *Janteloven* immediately helped me understand the strict environment I was experiencing. The rules show that Scandinavians fundamentally

---

103   "The Law of Jante—Explained," *ScandiKitchen* (blog), Scandikitchen
      Blomhoj, accessed March 21, 2021.

care about equality; they believe everyone should be and have *the same*. But even if everyone could be the same, that level of conformity would affect people differently. Equality is not the same as equity.

Around the fifth grade, I was a stickler for rules. I was the most annoying little girl in the classroom telling other kids what to do. On the rare occasion when I saw my mom drink—for example, on vacation in Mexico—I got up from my family's table, found my own booth in the restaurant, and dramatically rolled my eyes across the room at her all night. I didn't realize at the time how my own emotional instability was causing me to enforce structure in other people's lives.

Up until then, my family was picture perfect in my memory, but there were many adulthood complexities I didn't pick up on. My mom had worked as a chef at the preschool my sister and I attended so our family could afford the tuition. When she went back to work full-time at an insurance company—so our family would have guaranteed health and life insurance benefits—I started taking care of my own afternoon snacks. After the divorce, I lived with my mom full-time and saw my dad on Wednesday evenings and every other weekend.

At my old elementary school, I was popular. I was the smart girl whom people made friends with for help on their homework. My teachers pulled me out of the classroom for a weekly accelerated program; the kids in the class who tested highest in first, second, and third grade got to learn about probability, logic, and other advanced topics for an hour a week. I can't remember exactly how I felt at that time, but my friend in high school later told me how the program made him and the people left behind feel dumb. The school preened me to believe I was better or more capable than my classmates when I was only eight or nine.

In fourth grade, the school suggested my parents move me to Rogers Park Elementary to join the Highly Gifted program. I was excited about the new opportunity to learn. School was my favorite part of the day.

I asked for a challenge, and I got it. At ten years old, I had pages and pages of homework to complete every evening. I was already stressed about family and now, for the first time in my life, I was stressed about school. The kids in my new classroom weren't like the neighborhood kids. To attend Rogers Park, I had to bus to the whitest part of Anchorage; one of the neighborhoods where, up until the early 1980s, homeowners signed contracts stating: "No race or nationality other than those of the White or Caucasian race shall use or occupy any dwellings on any lot in said Subdivision."[104] After school I popped a Marie Callender's chicken pot pie in the microwave, ate it, and then ate another one before dinner. By sixth grade, I was four-feet, eleven-inches tall and weighed one hundred fifty pounds.

Everything was going wrong in my little life: my dad was growing ever distant, my mom was back to work full time, I was supposed to help my little sister. I moved schools hoping something—namely, the one thing that had always gone well for me—would work out. My personality was to show my vulnerability around very few people. When I did talk about my problems, I often framed them like, "X is wrong, but don't worry, I'm doing Y to fix it!" It's both my defense mechanism and simultaneous attraction to human energy that gives me a genuinely easygoing air.

---

104 Aurora Ford, "Redlining in Fairview," *Anchorage Press*, February 27, 2017.

It was spring break of sixth grade that my dad committed suicide. I had already missed the first few days back to school and I told my mom I refused to stay home; I would be okay as long as everything proceeded as normal. In the few minutes before class began, students milled around the classroom with our solar system models hanging from the ceiling. I pulled my friend at the time to the side.

"What did you do over spring break?" she asked.

"Well," I stared at my twiddling fingers. "I wanted to talk to you because my dad died."

She looked at my face for exactly two seconds before responding, "You liar."

I fought back tears for many days thereafter. I felt alone in those classes. Actually, suicide was (and continues to be) all too common in the North. One hundred sixty-six other Alaskans took their own lives in 2008, at a per capita rate twice as high as the US average.[105] As far as I knew, these systemic problems weren't affecting other, primarily white students in my class.

As the years dragged on, bussing was eliminated for high school students. Teachers stopped talking about how smart I was and began to gossip about my behavior. During freshman year, the counselor threatened to drop me from the program because of my grades (although I graduated in the top 10 percent of my class). Systematically, all the students of color dropped out one by one. At graduation there were only a handful of people of color, many of them mixed like me, in the program of about fifty people. In *the fifth most diverse high school in the United States.*

---

105 Statewide Suicide Prevention Council, "Alaska Suicide Facts and Statistics" (Anchorage: Alaska Department of Health and Social Services, accessed February 28, 2021).

For much of her childhood, Anna was the only *mørkhudet* (dark-skinned) person in her small-town elementary school. One Black boy graduated from the sixth grade when she was in first grade. It wasn't until eighth grade that she had a class with another person of color. She was bullied often and mercilessly up through school, but adults did not believe her.

One boy in her eleventh-grade friend group, often drunk at high school parties, continually harassed Anna. One day he followed her and her best friend into a bathroom, locked himself inside, and blocked the entrance. He poked Anna in the shoulder and taunted them to kiss: "Kyss da så låse æ opp døra." *Just kiss already and I'll unlock the door.* Later, he told her that it was "just a joke" and he hadn't attacked her. But she still felt the place where his finger imprinted on her shoulder.

When she told the school about his actions, they didn't acknowledge it as bullying: *He just likes you because you're* "eksotisk," *exotic.*

"I'm white on the inside," Anna would insist. That's what she told me anyway. Norwegian-ness and whiteness are conflated; *ethnic Norwegians* are expected to be fair-skinned with blond hair.[106] But what about the over four hundred thousand non-Europeans living in Norway? Upon first glance, Norwegians couldn't accept that dark-skinned, dark-haired Anna could share a culture with them.

Generally, Norwegians assumed Anna was part of an immigrant family, so she strayed from telling people she was

---

106 Tony Sandset, *Color that Matters: A Comparative Approach to Mixed Race Identity and Nordic Exceptionalism* (New York: Routledge, 2019), 57.

adopted to avoid rude judgments. Although she has lived with her Norwegian parents in Norway since she was one year old, her own extended family still asked her "how to speak Indian" at holidays and reunions. When she worked as a teacher at a preschool, her coworkers talked very slowly because "møøørkhuuudeeen dooon't taaalk tooo goood."

Friends just gaslighted her when she told them her experiences as a person of color in Norway: "Ikke vær dramatisk, det lille extra." Don't be dramatic. *Det lille extra*—a little extra—was the nickname her high school friend group gave her. When people don't want to hear you, they belittle you.

One evening Anna strode into the *kollektiv* living room distressed. She loved working with toddlers but couldn't find full-time work in the field. She had started a new job vending sandwiches and coffee at the airport a few weeks ago, and she was still wearing her collared polo with the airport logo.

"What's going on?" I asked her.

"Today was a mess at work," she sighed. She'd told me that, even compared to the *kindergarten* job, there were too many Karens to deal with at the airport. (Anna watches a lot of TikTok and devours American media much more studiously than me.) Too many oblivious questions and gross interactions.

Today she didn't make a sandwich quickly enough. A balding, red-nosed man dinged the client bell eight times in a row. She brought his toasted ham and cheese on a metal pan with both hands.

"Sorri, sorri, comming," Anna called out in Norwegian. She wiped her brow and rang up his order. "Det blir 48 kroner." That is six dollars.

"Så flink du er å snakke norsk," he accused. "Hvor er du fra?" *You speak good Norwegian. Where are you from?*

She lifted her head and stared into his face, deadpan. "I've lived here my whole life."

His nose reddened even more; his forehead sank toward his eyebrows.

"Nei, det tror jeg ikke på." *No, I don't believe that.* His head shook fervently. "Give me the sandwich."

Anna slid the sandwich across the counter and forced a cheery, "Hade bra!" *Goodbye!*

"Go back to where you came from," he spat.

Anna froze, hands midair, mouth closed. The other customers in line looked on. She wasn't surprised; she'd been used as an outlet for someone else's frustration before. But what had she done to deserve it?

"It isn't just at the airport," Anna told me back at the *kollektiv*. "Norwegians can be really racist. Especially older ones."

Anna's mom begged her to get another job. She was appalled at the stories her daughter brought back from work. She submitted applications on her behalf at other storefronts. She even brought her a job offer from a local cafe.

"What do you want to do for a job?" I asked.

"I'm like a hopeless person who has no idea what she wants to do," she sighed. Her eyes were wet. "I want—well, what we call it in Norway—is a normal *A-4 liv.* I want to be happy, drink juice in the morning, work a regular job, and have an apartment with a cat…"

An A-4 life, like an A-4 sized sheet of paper, would be standard, normal. She strived for that.

"Just, like, stability," I summarized.

"Yes. And I don't think things will change if I switch. I told my mom it wasn't just the airport. It's at school, around family… At home." Her big eyes turned toward me. "I just don't get how you do it. You seem like you always have it all together and perfect all the time."

Since childhood, I've been uber-conscious of other people's emotions and aimed to serve them. I learned to talk a lot and be very genuine while revealing little about myself. I wonder how I got this way. It troubles me that, surrounded by white classrooms and white adult mentors, I learned in my childhood to serve them at the expense of myself. There is a reason I never felt able to ask for help. I felt the need to project positivity without anger or grief at every moment— even when I *needed* to be angry or grieve.

Freshman year of high school, I felt safe enough around my new friends to talk about what happened to my dad. I had moved districts since middle school, and I felt these friends deserved to know more about me. When I finally opened up about his death, I told them we hadn't seen each other for a few months beforehand. He had relapsed, but never let me see him in that state.

A group of three or four of us huddled in the dimly lit computer lab after class. After a few moments, one of the other mixed kids from my class spoke up. His response: "It's okay, Michaela, all Blacks are criminals."

The others around me chuckled quietly, but I didn't join in.

"*What* did you just say?" I demanded.

"Chill out," he laughed, dark curls bouncing around his face. "It's just a joke."

I had to directly confront those stereotypes often. They were light humor to people in my gifted classes but informed the basic assumptions these young people would carry through life. Those stereotypes about Black identity are the reason so many Americans still don't believe in systemic racism, or that mass incarceration is a problem. America's racism has always been paired with criminalization. If it wasn't, people might start to suspect that racism is a problem.[107]

It wasn't until much later, in college, that I learned the history behind mass incarceration. For a long time, I didn't know those taunts were unfair. I was so immersed in whiteness, there were very few people I could turn to for understanding.

I would say my biggest weakness is a double-sided coin. Heads: People I'm close to have communicated that showing myself is not safe, so I project positivity and togetherness. Tails: I don't show enough of myself to grow supportive, intimate friendships that *make me* feel safe.

At the same time that I was dealing with my dad's passing, Anna struggled with her family over 3,300 miles across the Arctic Ocean. Her mom and dad fought often, loudly, and belittled each other to their daughter. Their divorce process lasted from the time she was nine until she was twelve. When they finally split, Anna felt safer at her mom's house because there were rules and structure. Her parents each vied separately for her attention, talking the other down and bribing her with gifts. Anna didn't want to let anybody down, but she hadn't felt like she had a real home since her parents divorced.

Throughout her final years of high school, Anna lived with her dad and younger brother, who was also adopted from India. They did not get along.

"He has abandonment issues. I do, too, a little," she told me. Anna was a baby when she came to Norway, and her brother had survived with his five-year-old brother as unhoused orphans until being separated from him and adopted at age

---

107 Angela Davis, *Are Prisons Obsolete?* (New York: Seven Cities Press, 2003), 28-34.

three. Abandonment issues are typical for people who were adopted or lost a parent at a young age.

On the first day they met, Anna's parents pushed their children toward each other until they were nose to nose. Without a word, he hoisted a hairbrush in his fist and jabbed her in the stomach.

"And he never stopped," she said.

He bullied her at home. Racism at school, isolation at home, and natural insecurities—exacerbated by two months without sunlight in the cold, polar night—made a harrowing combination. When she started saying the word *depresjon* to her parents, her brother cornered her in the bathroom. He was close enough that she could smell the taco pizza on his breath.

"You should just kill yourself." He smirked.

Anna's brother had lighter skin and more wealthy friends than her. He always wore designer clothes and drove a BMW purchased by their parents. Looks were important to him, though he hadn't had to fund it himself. Anna complained that he was never expected to have the responsibilities she did. She kept a job ever since she was fourteen and paid rent to her mom, not because her mom demanded so, but because she felt shame for taking from them.

I think all of us in the North—and maybe all of us, period—are dealing with internalized racism. Internalized racism: "the personal conscious or subconscious acceptance of the dominant society's racist views, stereotypes and biases of one's own ethnic group. It gives rise to patterns of thinking, feeling, and behaving that result in discriminating, minimizing, criticizing, finding fault, invalidating, and hating oneself while simultaneously valuing the dominant culture."[108]

---

108 Taking Action Against Racism in the Media, "Internalized Racism," October 17, 2016.

We have been told time and time again that we are slow, uncivilized, outsiders, worthless, criminals. We can hope to single handedly build loving, resilient relationships with ourselves. But it's also important to choose respectful relationships with people who will support us.

CHAPTER 9

RAKETTNATT

———

Racism is often spoken of as a barrier. Too infrequently
is it addressed as something that enables and permits.

—MICHAEL IVORY JR.

"Gå rundt," Anna shouted. She and I stood on the inside of
a flimsy-looking metal fence. We both wore neon vests and
brand-new black hoodies with the words "SPACE XXX" down
the sleeve, which we'd gotten from the RakettNatt volunteer
orientation earlier that day. The couple on the other side of
the fence walked toward us in raincoats, motioning to ask
whether they could walk through.

"Go roond!" I echoed.

Anna turned and shook her head at me. "I can't take
you anywhere."

"Go roond," I mouthed the letters carefully. "That's what
you said."

"Gåååååå *rundt*." She rolled her eyes and straightened her
vest. "Gosh."

RakettNatt is an annual music festival in Tromsø featuring
Norwegian artists alongside international stars like 2 Chainz,

A$AP Ferg, and Tove Lo. Remember, my strategy for making friends in Tromsø was getting involved in organized social activities—preferably those outdoors and with alcohol. When I heard of RakettNatt, I immediately signed up to volunteer. Anna and Nora also submitted a volunteer application so we could attend the concerts together on August 24 and 25, 2018.

On the day of our eight-hour volunteer shift, we bundled up in two layers of pants and boots and made the thirty-minute trek down to Tromsø *sentrum* for volunteer orientation. It was forty-some degrees, the sky was completely white-gray and opaque. In the North, fall is typically a wet and windy season characterized by increasingly dark and unfriendly weather. Today thick clouds casually mingled in the heavens, and rain seemed unlikely. We hoped the nice, dreary weather would persevere as we ducked into the rented office space for volunteers.

Forty or fifty of us sat around bench tables that you'd expect to see in a high school cafeteria. I squeezed in between Anna and a teenager with ear-length red hair. A hipster in her twenties was obviously in charge; she marched around the room calling out instructions while Anna translated in my ear.

"Som vil jobbe på inngangen?" she hollered. Ten hands shot up. She proceeded to point and choose volunteers: "Du, du og… du."

"What's happening?" I whispered to Anna.

"I think they're choosing jobs," she whispered back. On her left side, Anna patted Nora's leg.

"Som vil jobbe på kafeen?" she continued.

"Cafe?" Anna asked. We raised our hands, but not faster than anyone else.

"Du… du… værsågod… du… du. Tusen takk!" *You, you, here you go, you, you. Thank you!* She didn't see us in the back of the room.

"Greit," she continued. As volunteers filed outside to the festival, Anna, Nora and I were among the last people in the room. "Endelig… vi trenger 10 personer for sikkerhet." *Well, we need 10 people for…*

Anna turned to me. "Security?"

I shrugged and laughed. We climbed off the bench and walked to the volunteer coordinator, neither of us taller than five foot, three inches. I half expected them to turn us away. "Værsågod," she said. *Here you go.* She handed us each a neon vest and strapped festival bracelets on our wrists. Anna, Nora, and I followed another volunteer out the door to town square. Normally, Tromsø *sentrum* is a simple square laden with gray bricks on the coast of the island. There is a stone statue of a whaler at the base and a hot dog hut at the top, six-story tall buildings on either side, and the mayor's office is located one block up the hill. RakettNatt had transformed the square into something unrecognizable.

I craned my neck up toward the afternoon sky, a little less bright but still covered in clouds. Gigantic beach balls arranged like the solar system strung on ropes from one side of the square to the other. I admired Saturn's many rings, and my eyes followed the wire connecting the planet to Jupiter on the other side of the square. The sun hung large, bright, and orange over the center of the square. Near the front of the stage, the earth dangled parallel to spotlights. With the square fenced off up to the mayor's office, the outdoor venue was big enough for ten thousand people. A large bar area vended *øl og vin*—beer and wine. A professional stage covered half the square.

When the volunteer dropped Anna, Nora, and me at our security post, she handed Nora a walkie talkie to communicate with the rest of the group. She proceeded to give instructions.

"What did she say?" I asked when the volunteer walked away.

"Don't let people exit through here. Everyone must exit through the...," Anna stuttered and glanced at Nora for assistance.

"Main entrance," Nora finished. "And only let them in when they have a pink wristband." Nora pointed at the sign posted on the inside of the fence: pink wristbands for staff, blue for people whose apartment entrances are inside the concert area, purple for weekend-pass holders, and yellow for tonight's performance only.

We were stationed immediately off stage right. We could walk a few meters from the fence to watch the concert or peer through the fence to see celebrities drive backstage. On the inside, there was a Norwegian convenience store and a bar called Heidi's behind us.

At first there wasn't much traffic at our post. One resident inside the square flashed their blue bracelet at us before we pushed the fence aside to let her in. A few people came by the fence asking if they could walk through to the bus stop by the mayor's office.

"Gå rundt," Anna told them.

One man got angry, stormed up to the fence and yelled in Anna's face when she told him to go around: "Fuck du!" Nora told us that passing drivers often yelled obscenities at her construction job for inconveniencing their commute.

I studied the scene the whole night: festival goers marching up to the fence and barking orders, Anna and Nora communicating with them. There was a blatant disrespect for Anna, specifically. If they weren't yelling at or physically assaulting her, they spoke slowly as if she was dumb or unable to speak Norwegian.

After an hour, the main entrance opened, and festival goers began to fill the inside of the square. Norwegian artists started the festival off. Thousands more wristbands entered the square throughout the evening in advance of the closing act: A$AP Ferg.

"Honestly, I'm not looking forward to A$AP Ferg," I told Anna and Nora.

"You don't like him?" Anna asked.

"It's not that," I said. Anna had taken over communication and a brown-haired man approached her from the crowd before I could explain. He demanded to leave, but we were told not to let anyone exit the fence.

"Du må gå rundt," Anna declared, squaring her shoulders and staring into his face.

When Anna put her foot down in front of a grown Norwegian man, he decided he needed to put her in her place. He looked her up and down, grabbed hold of her shoulders, squeezed them and hoisted her into the air. He turned ninety degrees and released his grip, then walked past her out of the gap through the side of the gate. All I could do was stare and gasp in the seconds-long exchange.

"Satan!" Nora cursed him through the fence, pronounced the Norwegian way.

I was feeling increasingly fed up with this crowd of rowdy, drunk, and privileged festivalgoers (after all, the festival pass cost 1599 NOK, about US $200).

As the sky started to go dark, the RakettNatt planets began to glow. The whole square lit up in flashing pinks and yellows. Thousands of blonds and brunets milled around waiting for the rapper to go onstage. Crowds of five and ten at a time stumbled into the convenience store for drunchies, while other people lingered across the street from the fence for a free concert. Empty beer cans crunched under my feet. A few people climbed onto their friends' shoulders before being told to get down while American rap music echoed around Tromsø *sentrum*.

A club horn blared—*do do do-doooo*—and A$AP Ferg's hypemen ran onstage from the back. They whooped into the mic, "What's up, Norway!" Soon, Ferg was deep in his set. Dressed in a black and red flannel buttoned up to his chin, they played "Work," "Dump Dump," and "Shabba." The crowd jumped up and down with the music. My ear drums felt like they might not survive this concert. When "Plain Jane" came on, I braced myself.

I saw a lot of perfectly quaffed blond and brunette heads bobbing above the sea of people. Tall boys wore sunglasses at nighttime, track pants, brand-name hoodies and bomber jackets. A few girls I spotted had lip injections, slick-back ponytails and "boxer braids." The whole crowd bounced on their toes and yelled the lyrics. I closed my eyes and took deep breaths. It would be over soon.

"—NIGGA—!" I didn't lock eyes with anyone in the crowd. I don't remember looking at Anna or Nora for their reactions. Just the sea of people and their deafening cry:

"—NIGGA—!" All the white folks seemed to carry on without a care in the world. They smiled gleefully, crunching on the word with their grinning teeth.

"—NIGGA—!"

I turned to Anna and Nora after the song ended. I had too much energy and needed to walk around; my heart was racing.

"That is why I was worried about Ferg's concert," I said frantically, my eyes large and intent.

"Why?" Anna asked.

I gaped at her. "Because of all these white people saying the N-word."

It seemed obvious to me. I don't even say the word because I know I'm white-passing; I wouldn't want to offend someone who thinks I'm white. If I said it around white people in Alaska, they would think they could say it.

Nora looked at me with a bit of exasperation. "You're in Norway. It's not like in America."

I pulled away from the conversation and pretended to watch A$AP Ferg's next set. I couldn't very well tell her it *is* the same. I'd only been in Norway three months and didn't want to be like all the Americans who can only see the world from one perspective. Americans generally fail at integrating in foreign countries. We're too loud, too opinionated, not at all self-aware. It was my plan coming to Norway to experience the culture, without judgement.

But this topic felt all too familiar. During my freshman year of high school, my blonde English teacher in her thirties had to teach one of those "classic American novels" written by a white author who generously employed the N-word. She asked us all to read paragraphs, popcorn style, during class. Before we read the book, though, she asked the students to make a decision.

"I leave it up to you," she said, "whether to read the N-word aloud. As you know, the word has a wrought history. I expect you are all very intelligent and can decide for yourselves: If it's your turn to read when the word comes up, you choose what to do."

With our desks positioned around the class in a circle, I could see each student's face as they said the word. All the students but two were white. The freckled brunette girl with the curly hair said it monotone, as if it didn't affect her. The mousy-haired girl who bullied me in fifth grade said it, too. I watched the same guy whose dog I took care of mouth it as he lifted his eyes to meet mine. Altogether, my class said "nigger" twenty-six times.

Afterwards, still arranged in a circle, the teacher asked the class to discuss whether they felt differently about using the word. Each student said why they felt it was okay. The most popular reason: It's just words in a book. I'd heard that excuse from my classmates before when, at parties or in cars headed outside school grounds for lunch, they yelled "nigga" along with their music.

"Why can't I say it? It's just a song. Things are different in Alaska, Michaela."

My Alaskan peers typically argued that racism didn't exist in Alaska because African Americans were never enslaved there. Looking back, that was a naive, easily defeated argument. All you have to do is *listen to Black people* to hear their experiences with racism: the racist housing covenants rampant in the very neighborhoods these children went to school in, the murders of Black people by police, the disproportionate number of us in prison. Racism enables white people to simply ignore us when we point out inequity.

When you listen to a *mørkhudet* person talk about their experiences in Norway, it's very clear that Norwegians act racist too.

Alcohol did not amount to friendship at Rakettnatt. However, it did a few weeks later.

Tromsø boasts the most bars per capita in all of Norway.[109] I frequented a wine bar on the Walking Street with outdoor seating laden with furs and blankets. I also took advantage of student discounts at Driv, drank beer over games of Putt-Putt

---

109 Malek Murison, "A Guide to Tromsø," Norway Travel Guide, accessed March 28, 2021.

minigolf at Storgata Camping, and sat around crowded booths at Agenturet Øl og Vinbar.

Fun Pub was my favorite bar. It was the only club where people would dance, and entrance was also free. The patronage included a mix of ethnic Norwegians and international patrons. The DJ played a combination of 2000s American hip hop and Norwegian pop that my drunk self adored. On the best nights, dozens of people from around the world shook their booties on the ten-foot square dance floor tucked in the back of the bar.

One night I was buying a beer at the Fun Pub when I met Chilon. He leaned on the wall near the bar, over two meters tall, broad at the shoulders and skin deep as mahogany. For only the second time in Tromsø, a stranger approached me.

"Hvor du fra?" Chilon asked. He bent forward and projected over the music and shouting Norwegians.

"I'm from Alaska," I said. I was beginning to grasp common Norwegian phrases, even though I couldn't speak it without being made fun of. Chilon's voice sounded different than a north Norway accent. "What about you? Are you Norwegian?"

"Nei," he replied in Norwegian. "Don't call me that. I am Norwegian on documents only."

I laughed out loud. "Well then, what's your story?"

Over the glasses clinking, girls squealing, and—was that Shakira I heard playing on the dance floor?—Chilon said, "I speak Norwegian, I know their culture, but I'm Black. And proud."

Chilon was from Congo. He said he remembered the time when he lived in a big family apartment with his parents. He could still recollect the taste of sweet candies they used to give him after returning from work. He missed the feeling of belonging in a country that was his own, before the guns came. He remembers clutching the legs of a table and holding his breath as soldiers arrived to kill his people.

When Chilon was six, he escaped to Zambia with his parents and siblings without documents. Refugee control would send them back to a warzone if they were caught. Chilon learned to speak English there on top of his native Swahili. By adulthood, his French would slip away. It began to be replaced by Norwegian when he moved there from Zambia at the age of nine. After growing up with his family in southern Norway, Chilon trained at the joint Norwegian-American military base in northern Norway (Bodø) and worked to earn a flat in Tromsø.

Nearly twenty years later, Norwegian was his most frequently used language and small, coastal towns in the Arctic were the home he imagined for his future. He appreciated the quiet that permeated the town and countryside in northern Norway. The deafening fireworks on New Year's still made him jump. He enjoyed solitary time; it's then that he could develop his self-identity.

"You know, a bank teller once told me I should take a Norwegian name," he told me, arm propped on the bar. Later, he said his round cheeks made him look like a young Muhammed Ali.

The bank teller suggested he should change his name to "Kjell Arne," "Chilon" Norwegianized. Smiling, he projected over the music and asked, "So you know what I said to her? I said, 'What about you? Would you change yours into African name?'" A laugh escaped his belly as he recalled it. "She said no, and she knew my answer, too."

Chilon's peers say his biggest flaw is that he's too full of himself. He did not want to be singled out and bullied for the color of his skin or told to change fundamental parts of his being on a regular basis so he would seem more Norwegian. Being seen and respected as himself would have meant equity for Chilon. However, that equity came in direct contest with "equality" for Norwegians.

Norwegians don't talk about this kind of discrimination as racism. Instead, the majority of society thinly veils their contempt as a debate about social and national cohesion in the face of mass migration.[110] But Chilon knew better. No matter whether he changed his name or tried to act more Norwegian, the way he looked would always identify him as *utlending*.

"I don't like having to constantly ask Norwegians for approval without getting it," Chilon said. "I have to be what I feel I am."

His feelings were all too familiar to me. When you're surrounded by people who have different worldviews than yourself, the fact that other people disagree with you necessarily doesn't mean you are wrong. It just means you have to keep a stronger resolve in who you are.

After having experienced over a thousand white people blissfully yelling slurs, it felt empowering to meet a friend who stood firm in his identity despite the culture of whiteness around him. Chilon became one of my closest friends in Tromsø. I appreciated that he was thoughtful, a great listener, and was confident in being himself. On weekends and over the holidays, he regularly introduced me to his friends. He brought me to parties unannounced, unabashedly breaking Norwegian social rules.

"Michaela, we hang out sometime?" he asked, the first time we met.

---

110 Sindre Bangstad, "The Racism that Dares not Speak its Name," *Intersections. East European Journal of Society and Politics* 1 (2015): 49-65.

"I'm going on a trip next week," I told him at the time, "but maybe after I get back?"

In the next few months, I wouldn't be spending so much time in Tromsø with Anna, Nora, or Chilon. The summer vacation season was long over, and Norwegians and Sámi alike were back to work. The festivals would soon be over too. Fall in Sápmi was calving season, and I'd been invited to visit some reindeer herds.

CHAPTER 10

ALVIÐRA

Ironically, by fighting to save the seals, all these
[environmental] groups have inadvertently put all the
Arctic animals, not to mention us humans, at higher risk.
—ALETHEA ARNAQUQ-BARIL

The least American food I've ever eaten is probably sheep face.
When I was twenty and studying abroad in Iceland, I stayed
with an eccentric couple named Matthildur, a local feminist
organizer with blue-streaked hair, and Guðmunder, a six foot
tall, completely bald bass player. While Matta usually strayed
from the funky traditional Icelandic foods, Gummi loved
them. He bought us the sheep's head from the local grocery
store, where we wandered through the aisles until we found
a freezer full of them all wool-less and shrink-wrapped in
plastic. After baking it for an hour, my Icelandic host parents
served the angular mug on a plate with sugared mashed pota-
toes. The sheep's head had been sliced in half and the brains
and horns removed, so all that remained were two halves of
a skull covered in a thin layer of rich meat. The nose, eyes,
and tongue were edible, they told me. Instead, I peeled away

a piece of brown skin and removed a little forkful of pink, tender meat from the cheek.

You'd never believe that, just a few weeks earlier, I still considered myself a vegetarian.

After my freshman year of college, I came back to Alaska a self-proclaimed pescatarian. As someone who cares about climate change, I deluded myself about food's role in the mix until an Introduction to Environmental Science & Policy class. I learned there are all sorts of problems with America's agro-industrial complex. For one, industrial food production relies on a sea of petroleum-based fertilizers. Cows produce methane, but they also consume crops, mostly corn—entire fields of edible plants that humans could be eating. Gram for gram of protein, beans require only 5 percent of the land area and carbon emissions that beef does.[111] I realized I couldn't continue putting agro-industrial meat in my body and call myself an environmentalist.

There is also a human rights dimension to agro-industrial complexes. Flying over eastern North Carolina in 2016, large brown rectangles splattered in between green farmland from my bird's eye view. I knew what they were from studying environmental racism at Duke: vats of pig manure. *Literal, open cesspools.* North Carolina farms raise about nine million pigs each year, but hog farms smell disgusting and tear down property prices.[112] Rather than upset wealthy neighbors, industrial pig farms are slotted for poor, usually Black communities. Industry says, "the solution to pollution is dilution," so pig farmers plug in industrial-size fans to blow the manure

---

111 Stephen Leahy, "Choosing Chicken Over Beef Cuts Our Carbon Footprints a Surprising Amount," *National Geographic*, June 10, 2019.

112 NC Pork Council, "Pork as a Passport: Food Unites Us," January 2, 2021.

off their properties. The putrid fumes infest surrounding homes, causing locals to suffer from higher blood pressure, asthma, constant nausea and respiratory problems.[113]

My resolve was firmer than ever not to buy meat. I had no problem with people eating meat; I had a problem with corporations exploiting people, animals, and the environment to profit off agro-industry. I called myself a flexitarian often because I ate meat if it would otherwise be wasted, like leftovers from a catered event at school.

When I arrived in Iceland, I knew I would have to eat some meat. Actually, my host mom was happy to cook pescatarian and we ate the same food most of the time. But before globalization, the most reliable food sources in the North were animals; fruit trees and vegetable vines don't grow in the snow, which could cover the ground from September to June. What the Arctic does have are large animals. Depending on where they live, people eat birds, caribou, sheep, and, yes, seals and whales.

I was the only person from the North on my study abroad program. The rest of the participants were outdoorsy, aspiring scientists traveling from small liberal arts schools on the east coast. Most of us were vegetarian or pescatarian, and a few were vegan. I got in an argument with one student who insisted that eating meat, even if meat has been the basis for your sustenance for generations upon generations, was wrong.

"Don't you agree, as a moral and sentient species, that we *all* have a moral obligation to not eat other animals?" he implored.

We were en route via water taxi for a class trip. His pale white skin reflected like a mirror off the boat's portholes.

---

113 Erica Hellerstein and Ken Fine, "A Million Tons of Feces and an Unbearable Stench: Life Near Industrial Pig Farms," *The Guardian*, September 20, 2017.

Earlier in the year we'd traveled to Greenland, where he loudly declined a magnanimous brunch of delicacies like smoked salmon, fresh caviar, thinly sliced seal, and whale meat on crackers. Today he was ticked off by my excitement about an upcoming trip to see my host family's sheep in Alviðra.

"No, I don't," I retorted, holding his gaze. "I think the rate at which you emit carbon dioxide to ship plant-based foods to the Arctic, you'll kill whales just as quickly with climate change."

Industrialization and commercialization have ushered in a new geological time period, the Anthropocene, and caused the sixth great extinction of species on Earth. In fact, the most geologically supported start date for the Anthropocene is 1610: made possible by the white supremacists' slave trade and seizure of the Americas, the exchange of plants and animals across the Atlantic forever changed Earth's geologic history.[114] By using least-cost resources and labor from other continents, Europeans created a pattern of overextending ecological limits to sustain economic growth. Industry unhampered created the catastrophic collapse of Pacific cod, sea turtles in Mexico, and bowhead whales in the Arctic. Consider that, today, entire sections of the Amazon rainforest continue to be cleared for soybean crops to feed farm animals and the growing plant-based foods movement.[115] The loss of species, combined with drastic land use change and temperature increases within only four hundred years, marks a very new era in Earth's history.

Eating meat is not our biggest environmental problem. Overconsumption and land use change—which often comes

---

114 Simon L. Lewis and Mark A. Maslin, "Defining the Anthropocene," *Nature* 519, no. 7542 (March 2015): 171–180.

115 Yale School of Forestry & Environmental Studies, "Soy Agriculture in the Amazon Basin," *Global Forest Atlas*, January 2, 2021.

hand in hand with erosion of land ownership for Black and Indigenous peoples—are. If you act as if all the world's resources are for your consumption, you will exploit them. If your primary goal is profit and continuous growth, you will not seek to compensate for the harms and externalities associated with your business. Therefore, the "tragedy of the commons" is a western one. The core morals behind under-regulated capitalism should be questioned—not the morals of meat-eating Arctic peoples.

It struck me as distinctly colonial to show up in Greenland, home of Inuit, and Iceland, which had also been colonized by Denmark, and declare your own moral superiority. On a larger scale, Greenpeace and PETA activists had done this to Inuit seal hunters since the 1960s. The campaigns led the European Union to ban seal products and ultimately ruined the reputation of sealskins in fashion. Inuit people had been hunting seals sustainably for millennia, and the supplemental sale of skins made up a large part of the Inuit economy in Canada. Not only did incomes crash in the Canadian Arctic, but the rates of suicide skyrocketed.[116] Anti-meat eater attitudes had ruined lives before, so I was not fond of the insult on my host family.

See, Matta's family were sheepherders. Every year in August, they gathered all their friends and family, trekked into the fjords together, found the sheep marked as their own, and chased them downhill until the whole herd ended up at Alvidra. At the barn there, they would be sheared, chosen for breeding, and selected for slaughtering. Their parents had taught them to do it, as had the many generations before them. They were no strangers to any aspect of the sheep's anatomy.

---

116 Alethea Arnaquq-Bari, *Angry Inuk* (Toronto: Unikkaat Studios, National Film Board of Canada and EyeSteelFilm, 2016), Vimeo rental.

The fall that I stayed in Iceland, my host family invited me to the annual slaughter.

"We don't bring every student," Matta told me. She opened her home to a couple American students per year, but some were judgmental. Many people who came to study environmental science in Iceland were vegetarians.

The day I was invited to attend the slaughter, we pulled up at Alvidra—Matta's family farm—in her SUV at 11 a.m. The family's home nestled into a sloping hill toward the ocean, its paint weathered, but its log-cabin interior well maintained. We hopped out, stretched our small jackets to block the rain, and ran inside. Matta slid on a full waterproof suit and I picked up a heavier coat from the work clothes in the garage. On the way out the front door, rainy photos from the decades hung across the hallway of Matta's parents, grandparents, and her sister's family, who inherited the sheep. We then drove down to the barn, where Matta's family had finished corralling them.

Matta parked in the slushy mud above the barn, and our boots made squishy sounds as we traipsed downhill to enter near the sheep room. The wooden slats of the barn made up at least three cavernous, wooden rooms: a large, short-ceilinged room where one hundred or more sheep huddled; a smaller room adjacent the opposite wall for slaughtering; and, leading from there, a drafty room for hanging the meat.

Her family bustled around the barn, discussing in Icelandic which sheep were fit for eating, which were ready for mating, which seemed sick or elderly. Matta's brothers stood among them, then hooked an arm under each sheep chosen for slaughter and walked it toward an opaque pen in the slaughter room where four or five sheep milled around.

Those given another year to live baa-ed to each other and nestled up to their mothers; one dominant male, almost doubly large as the females circling around him, butted heads with another testosterone-flooded sheep. The creatures were all different shades and colors.

"Most herders like the white wool because it can be dyed many colors," Matta told me, laughing. "My family likes the black sheep, the brown wool. I don't know why; it's just our way." Although Iceland's population was 99 percent white and 96 percent Icelandic, I noticed that Matta's family hung a painting of Black Jesus above the dining room table at Alviðra.

For now, I held on to the fence between me and the sheep with one hand and fed grass to nearby sheep with the other; kneeling toward the fence, our eyes could meet. Two sheep inched closer and accepted hay from my outstretched fingers; their teeth grinded in clockwise circles. The little sheep was brown and its mom, Matta told me, was the white creamy one with black spots around her eyes. Their fur was frizzy, wavy, and nearly touched the dirt barn floor.

"Would you grab more grass to feed the sheep?" Matta asked. Meanwhile, her brothers wrestled a few more males to the slaughter room.

They killed the first four sheep while I was gone. Two brothers at a time would lead one out of the pen and lay its head on a platform. A third man placed a columnar tube on the sheep's skull. When he pressed the trigger, a bolt of compressed air quickly shot a needle in its brain.

As I began to wonder what was happening in there, Matta came into the sheep's waiting area to make sure I still wanted to watch the slaughter. I wasn't truly sure how I'd react; blood thumped through my veins so forcefully that I heard it in my ears. I'd never actually watched a slaughter outside the industrial processing facilities in documentaries. But I believe humans are natural animal eaters. Logically, I knew that shopping at Costco was much worse for the planet.

I'm Alaskan; I'm the Fish Killer, I thought.

"I'm ready," I told her.

Matta's sole job throughout the process was calming and caring for the sheep to be slaughtered. She bent down and petted each of them, running her fingers through their wooly hair. At first, I helped her. An opaque plastic fence lined the pen around us. It kept the sheep from seeing their brothers pass.

Matta motioned that I go stand nearer the main event and learn. Her brother began to use the needle tube.

"Air pressure change ends the sheep's life immediately so he doesn't feel pain," Matta's brother said, when I asked if it hurt. The needle moved quickly enough to make the sheep unconscious as it passed on.

Like chickens with their heads cut off, the sheep's nerves continued running through their bodies. Two men wrestled the sheep's now dead body onto a wooden platform while it flailed like a bucking stallion. One of the men used his knife to remove the animal's head, and only then did the nerves cease.

Though it took a lot of force, Matta's brothers could remove the sheep's skin from its muscles and organs with their bare hands. One of them made insertions near the sheep's ankles, the other dunked his arm into a water bucket up to his elbows, then slipped his fingers into the space between the sheep's skin and body.

The fatty casing around its organs and muscles was folded into a cake to dry and use like lard. In addition to the meaty parts of the sheep, the testicles were saved as a delicacy that would turn the most profit. The horns were sawed off and saved for decoration and jewelry. The bones were kept for broth. The heads were drenched in a layer of salt to be cured before freezing and selling to the public.

In total, twenty sheep were slaughtered: nineteen males, one female. Matta frowned when we met each other's eyes again.

"This is a very sad day," she sighed.

The mood in the barn was somber. Though the sheep roam the mountains freely most of the year, Matta had gotten to know them. She knew their personalities, had given them names. Matta's ten-year-old niece lost her favorite sheep this year, whom she would mourn. This was the worst day of work, but still part of the job if you want to eat and provide for your family.

Before Iceland, the only vision I had of animal slaughterhouses were from American documentaries: thousands of cows hanging from gigantic metal hooks, blood dripping onto white floors and splattered on white uniforms and hair nets. Impersonal, industrial. Because of those images, I had worried I might throw up when I saw the butcher slice into the sheep's body.

But here, emotions and morals were not separate from the sterile factory environment; they were integral to the work. Food was not the meal on your plate, but the animal you raised from calfhood. These sheep were raised locally, required fewer fossil fuels than if industrially produced, lived a largely independent life on the land like their ancestors, and provided income for a caring family. When my host family offered to cook a sheep's head, I knew it was much more wholesome than the food I would have eaten at home.

"My favorite," Gummi said with a thick Icelandic accent. His lips curled into a smile as he aimed his fork for the sheep's face, scooped out an eyeball, and slurped it down like an oyster.

A face is a personal body part, sure, but raising food should be a personal process. We've forgotten that in America. As a city girl, I didn't learn it until I visited Iceland. But among sheep herders, the truth was self-evident.

4

FALL-WINTER

CHAPTER 11

REINØYA

_____

We believe indigenous food culture and the practice of food
sovereignty in the Arctic is a means by which the possibilities
of an economic and societal development based on our own
resources, knowledge and collective strength can be fulfilled.

—EALLU

Identity is not just about the color of one's skin, but also about cultural differences and world views. Concepts like perpetual economic growth, exploration of frontiers, and ownership of land are embedded in western world views. Modern globalization and histories of European colonialism have entrenched these values in every corner of the globe, but they are not "innately human." The preference toward economic growth is a learned cultural bias.

As a non-Indigenous girl from the city, there were many things I could learn from North Sámi world views. After graduating with distinction from one of the top ten schools for environment and ecology in the world, I felt very knowledgeable about the natural environment. I had studied environmental peacebuilding and negotiation among graduate students. I sampled every field, from investigating the phylogeny of an *Azolla* fern, to helping rescue a beached turtle during a study-abroad course in Baja Mexico. I could explain the greenhouse gas effect like citing my ABCs. And if I saw someone litter, I was bound to confront them. These are some reasons why people at Duke dubbed me Mother Nature: I was more passionate and familiar with the outdoors than most people I knew.

I have to admit that, among reindeer herders, my knowledge paled drastically in comparison.

The Saami Council, which represents the Sámi nation internationally via member organizations from across Finland, Sweden, Norway, and Russia, chaired the Indigenous Peoples' Secretariat while I was a Fellow there. A few colleagues from the Saami Council and their family members at the Association of World Reindeer Herders (an Observer organization to the Arctic Council) invited me to visit their reindeer herd at Reinøya, *Reindeer Island,* in mid-September. I jumped at the opportunity.

I arrived with my work colleagues around noon on a Friday. We'd been driving north from Tromsø for five hours, pulled the car onto a ferry boat, floated across a fjord, and bumpily steered up a single-lane dirt road. Ole-Ante Turi, then the Saami Council representative in the Arctic Council's Conservation of Arctic Flora and Fauna Working Group, met us at a cabin on high ground at Reinøya.

"You missed all the hard work!" Ole-Ante had laughed.

Though I'd emailed with him, this was the first time we met in person. He was gregarious and calm, an inch or two taller than me with a white lasso wrapped around his waterproof jacket more than twenty times. Over the past four days, he and his family, the Turi *siida,* had nudged thousands of reindeer into their annual corral place on foot and snow machine. While there always needed to be at least one herder with the reindeer, this weekend required all hands on deck. We were supposed to help corral, but obviously we were late.

Just as in Iceland, I missed the dirty, difficult part of herding the animals to slaughter. As Ole-Ante led us toward the corral, I hoped I'd have the opportunity to be useful to herders one day. Very few people can say they've been among real, live sheep and reindeer herds, and I basked in gratitude while enjoying the scenery. We hiked nearly an hour from there inside muddy four-wheeler tire tracks, avoiding the acres of squishy, crowberry- and willow-laden ground around us. Each panting breath sent a puff of steam into the air.

As we topped the hill, my eyes popped at the massive herd of reindeer swirling around a fenced area: a circular pen staked with six-foot-tall birch stalks and wrapped in a grid of wire. At least a thousand deer sprinted around each other in a circular pattern like a dog follows its own tail. They trotted over permafrost hills where water had turned to ice and expanded underground. And beyond there, *lavvus* shaded in the glare of sunlight dipping toward the horizon behind them. Fall was naturally the time when male reindeer began to rut and collect harems of over thirty females each. Reindeer herders knew to take advantage of this season by herding harems toward each other and into a corral.

Ole-Ante led us toward the *lavvus*, where four or five people in the *siida*, the family's traditional reindeer herding collective, rested on reindeer hides around a blazing fire. Everyone here knew each other much longer than me, as many were Ole-Ante's cousins, aunts, and uncles. The exception were a few of my colleagues, who had a decades-long and trusting relationship with the family. There were children running around, as well as dogs with heavy reindeer bones tied to their collars to keep them from running away.

I sat next to the oldest man, spry with deep smile wrinkles and adorned in a three-pointed, blue felt traditional hat. He slid his seven-inch knife in his windbreaker, wiped his hand on his pant leg, and reached out a slightly bloody hand.

"Bures," he said.

Assuming Bures was his name I took his hand and smiled, kneeling my head a bit. "Michaela."

He burst into laughter and with the other hand slapped his knee, stretched out to the side on the thick brown hide. He told me his name was Johan Mathis, Ole-Ante's uncle, and I was supposed to say *bures*—hello in northern Sámi—in return. Although I had learned a lot about Norway by now, I still had a lot to learn about Sápmi. Indigenous languages are one of the richest ways elders impart their knowledge on people in the community.

"Coffee?" Johan Mathis asked. "Try it with a bit of reindeer fat. That's the secret ingredient to keep you warm."

He fiddled with the metal kettle strung over the fire pit. When it had boiled over the fire for a few minutes, he transferred coffee to a wooden mug, a *guksi*. Johan removed his knife from his belt and dried reindeer from his pocket, then sliced a bit of white fat into the deep brown coffee. I sipped while it steeped inside and, at my new friend's suggestion, chewed on the rich fat to keep me warm.

I mimicked the way Johan Mathis sat with his bent knees to the side and nestled the *guksi* in the crook of my legs on the prickly reindeer hide. For a while, I watched two women kneel over a body for cleaning. All the parts of the reindeer could be used for something important. The hide sewn with sinew from the spine became *beaska*, a tunic suited for winter. *Suovasbiergu*, smoked meat, and *mális*, meat cooked to perfection with only water and salt, are common meals with more nutritional value and less health risks than American beef.[117] Even the animals' stomachs could be used as pots. Reindeer blood contains vitamin C, the only local source for Indigenous peoples in the high latitudes from Sápmi to the Far East of Russia.[118]

Meanwhile, men and women alike stood, kneeled, and sat around the fire talking politics—specifically, their current struggles with the reindeer herding department of Norway.

"There used to be lots of families out on the tundra. We all used to travel with the herds. You could meet a wife out here. Not anymore," Johan Mathis lamented.

He spoke with perpetual humor and lightheartedness, despite the grief associated with the industrialization and loss of traditional reindeer herding. Even in my lifetime, I had watched the forests near my childhood home be bulldozed for new cul-de-sacs and witnessed the arrival of Walmart and many more chains to Alaska. I imagined what the tundra might have looked like when he was a boy: the sound of Sámigiella filling the *lavvu*; lots of spiky-haired children licking blueberries from their fingertips; couples bathing in the cool rivers they passed on annual migrations. Many of today's elders have witnessed a complete transformation of the Arctic in their lifetimes.

At the beginning of the twentieth century, the Norwegian state operated fifty boarding schools designed to separate

---

117 Máret Rávdná Buljo et al., "Sámi: Smoked & Cooked," in *EALLU: Indigenous Youth, Food Knowledge & Arctic Change*, ed. Philip Burgess (Guovdageaidnu/Kautokeino: International Centre for Reindeer Husbandry, 2017).

118 "Reindeer meat - a part of nature and Sami culture," Samer.se, accessed February 3, 2021.

school-age children from their *siidas*.[119] At school the children were not allowed to speak their own language. They were systemically taught that Norwegians were superior to Sámi; between the World Wars, the Norwegian Director of Schools said, "The few individuals who are left of the original Lappish tribe are now so degenerated that there is little hope of any change for the better for them. They are hopeless and belong to Finnmark's most backward and wretched population."[120] Some Sámi were subjected to Social Darwinist experiments that aimed to prove their racial inferiority.[121] Many children returned from boarding schools with shame and chose to settle in towns instead of herding nomadically.

To make matters worse, German Nazis occupied northern Norway during World War II, from 1940–1945. They scorched entire towns in Finnmark, disproportionately affecting Sámi home ownership.[122] Scandinavian governments subsequently increased security at their borders and made many families' reindeer migration routes illegal. It's amazing that, in 1946, Norwegian ethnographers noted reindeer-herding *siidas* still traveled along traditional migration routes as their ancestors did. However, those same ethnographers reported that such a practice was "out of date" and required radical modernization.[123]

---

119 Henry Minde, *Assimilation of the Sámi - Implementation and Consequences* (Ontario: Aboriginal Policy Research Consortium International, 2005).

120 Ibid.

121 Ibid.

122 Gáldu - Resource Centre for Rights of Indigenous Peoples, "From Norwegianisation to Sami movement - Recent history," 0:00-0:30, March 30, 2007.

123 Kathrine Ivsett Johnsen, Svein Disch Mathiesen, and Inger Marie Gaup Eira. "Sámi reindeer governance in Norway as competing knowledge systems: a participatory study." *Ecology and Society* 22, no. 4 (2017): 33.

To achieve that aim, the Storting, Norway's lawmaking body, signed two new reindeer husbandry acts into law in the late 1970s. These laws did not take into account the *siida* family structure, its customs, ethics, values nor boundaries. Scientists, rather than reindeer herders themselves, advised policies to increase meat production and cash incomes from reindeer.[124] The process of subverting Indigenous knowledge with science, called rationalization, totally transformed and mechanized reindeer herding in the post-war reconstruction years.[125]

For example, herders received cash for sending their animals to a western-style slaughterhouse in Guovdageaidnu, the Sámi town near the Turis' winter pastures. Unlike the women I had been watching, the slaughterhouse did not use all of the meat. It prioritized western cuts like tenderloin and packaged the meat for mass consumption across Norway. Traditionally, herders did the slaughtering themselves to preserve meat quality dependent on very particular slaughtering methods.

"The best quality meat doesn't start in the kitchen," Johan Mathis advised. The secrets to raise, slaughter, and prepare the best reindeer were found in *árbediehtu*, Sámi Indigenous knowledge. Indigenous knowledge is the intergenerationally inherited truths and facts and methods wrapped up in Indigenous languages and ways of being.

Over Johan Mathis' shoulder, some Turis surveyed reindeer from the inside of the fence area. They constantly observed individual reindeer's behavior and body to quickly detect illness. They discussed which ones were good for eating this year, which males needed to be vasectomized to increase their size, which calves should be marked by whom in the

124 Ibid.

125 Ibid.

family. The ones slaughtered had to be chosen based on the color of the hide, gender, and age in order to keep a diverse herd. The way the reindeer died was important, too. To ensure safe meat, the herder let the reindeer's body rest on the tundra for a certain time based on the weather and temperature.[126]

Sámi reindeer herders inherit generations upon generations of knowledge about how to safely care for and slaughter their animals, which contains invaluable knowledge about the Arctic environment. There are words in Arctic languages that have no translation into English and other majority languages. For example, there are over three hundred words in Northern Sámi describing types of snow; the most I've got are flurries, slush, sleet, blizzard, and snowflake.[127] Fortunately, descendants of Sámi speakers are the only ones with the right to herd reindeer in Norway.

"It is a saying," Johan Mathis mused, watching the clouds. "*Jahki ii leat jagi viellja*." He turned to me to explain, "The direct translation says that one year is not the next year's brother. It means that the years are not alike."

"There is no word for stability in our language," Ole-Ante said, nodding in agreement. "It is unwise to think about stability where the winters, spring, summer, and autumn are not alike. We need the knowledge to adapt to any situation that will need action. Flexibility is the key to success."

Even since we'd been sitting on the reindeer hides, strong winds began to flap the *lavvus'* loose canvas. In a region where two months of never-ending sunshine turned to two

---

126 Buljo et al., "Sámi: Smoked & Cooked," in *EALLU: Indigenous Youth, Food Knowledge & Arctic Change.*

127 Inger Marie Gaup Eira et al., "Snow cover and the loss of traditional indigenous knowledge," *Nature Climate Change* 8, no. 11 (November 2018): 924–936.

months of the sun never broaching the horizon, herders needed to be ready for any weather, storm, or circumstance. To maintain a robust herd, they must be able to relocate to different pastures when the weather doesn't allow feeding in predetermined areas.

But the state—made mostly of Norwegian people who could not herd reindeer or speak Sámi—increasingly seized control of the livelihood.[128] In public administration, stability and standardization are considered factors for success. When the government sets standardized, scientific controls on reindeer husbandry, they compete with principles behind *árbediehtu*. Regulation of reindeer husbandry results in a collision of worldviews.

Norway's Ministry of Agriculture and Food dictates reindeer husbandry legislation and Reindriftsforvaltningen, the Norwegian Reindeer Husbandry Administration, is responsible for implementing the State's policies on a day-to-day basis.[129] The government has dictated six different areas where reindeer herders have the right to seasonal grazing, migratory routes, calving areas, and rutting areas. These areas make up 40 percent of Norway's land mass. In order to control those lands, the government sets targets about weight, herd numbers, and density in the pastures; districts are required to comply.[130]

"They're like the department of fish and game. You can't trust them, they're always trying to reduce the catch limits and herd numbers," one of the younger people, Tuomma, said to me.

---

128 Sámi - Norway," International Centre for Reindeer Husbandry.

129 Ibid.

130 Johnsen, Mathiesen, and Gaup Eira, "Sami reindeer governance in Norway."

Tuomma, one of Ole-Ante's cousins, spent most of his time on the tundra. In the winter he drove a snowmobile ninety minutes between his house in Guovdageaidnu and his remote hut near the winter pastures. He spent weeks at a time in his isolated hut, woke at least once a night to check on his herd in winter, and monitored them 24/7 during fall calving. Having dedicated so much of his life to reindeer herding, you could call him an expert.

His sentiment was familiar to me. For example, a Traditional Ahtna Chief I worked with told me that state-sanctioned moose hunting conflicted with his tribe's traditional practices. Sport hunters liked to catch the biggest, strongest moose to mount a trophy on the wall. The Alaska Department of Fish & Game (ADF&G) took note and established that moose hunting was allowed with a permit during fall rutting season, when males were the most amped up with testosterone. However, Ahtna specifically chose not to hunt big moose so the strongest males could continue to have offspring. They only hunted males outside rutting season, when the meat would not be tainted with the taste of testosterone.

Regardless of the fact that Ahtna had hunted moose sustainably long before ADF&G was established, ADF&G cooperated with Alaska State Troopers to punish traditional hunters found to have taken moose outside state seasons. One traditional hunter in his tribe was shot and killed by police when Alaska State Troopers came to apprehend him.

The Alaska Department of Fish & Game proudly declares "Science First in the Last Frontier" on the front page of its website.[131] That clearly disregards the value of Indigenous knowledge systems in Alaska. Considering the ways in which

---

131 Alaska Department of Fish & Game, "Home," accessed February 2, 2021.

science has been used as a weapon against Indigenous peoples, it is *not* a welcoming moniker. Indigenous knowledge and science can solve massive systemic problems together, but, alone, science can be a narrow world view.

Many biologists in northern Norway complain about the massive scale of Sámi reindeer herding, according to their average targets for reindeer size, number of reindeer, and area of pasture lands. But they use generalized scientific targets to measure ecological balance, without treating Indigenous knowledge as a valuable contribution to the process. When the government finds a herder to have more reindeer than they deem sustainable, they order parts of the herd to be slaughtered. In 2012, the government ordered the slaughter of over forty thousand reindeer—more reindeer than the estimated twenty-five thousand Sámi speakers in Norway.[132,133]

Development is not always about growth. At the reindeer camp, environment was part of culture, inextricable from it. The ability of herders to continue working with reindeer and Arctic nature is quintessential to the continued development of northern Sámi culture, language, and ethnicity. Yet the focus on economic and scientific growth of reindeer husbandry is actively competing with continued development of *árbediehtu*.

Indigenous peoples have the right to self-determination: According to the United Nations' Declaration on the Rights of Indigenous Peoples they should be able to "freely determine

132 Tove Rømo Grande, "The Norwegian Government Ordered Massive Slaughterings of reindeer. Indigenous Sami Reindeer Herders Disagreed But Were Not Heard," Norwegian University of Life Sciences, February 25, 2020.

133 Marko Marjomaa, *North Sámi in Norway: An Overview of a Language in Context* (Mainz: European Language Diversity for All (ELDIA), 2012).

their political status and freely pursue their economic, social, and cultural development."[134] The primary avenue for self-determination in the reindeer herding bureaucracy is through *bruksregler*, internal management plans. Each herding district must develop and implement a plan for the reindeer herding administration designating their migration routes at given times of year, as well as the maximum herd numbers. But even within these plans, Sámi are required to adopt herding practices that ensure national targets set by Norwegian scientists.[135]

"One of the problems is that Sámediggi"—Sámi Parliament, the representative body that acts as an institution of cultural autonomy—"does not have ownership or control over land," Ole-Ante said. The Sámi Parliament has autonomy over issues that only concern Sámi. Issues of land and industrial development concern society at large, so the Sámi people only have consultation rights. When Sámi reindeer herders' desires counter those of Norwegians, the long, expensive legal process makes it difficult for reindeer herders to oppose industrial development in their grazing lands.

"The land is the basis for the Sámi culture," Johan Mathis, his uncle added. "Without land, the culture will disappear."

It was clear to me that Ole-Ante was practiced at explaining the concept of Sámi rights to non-Sámi. Many of us westerners would not understand intuitively, and that is part of the problem. He spoke in a matter-of-fact tone as he continued:

"My driving ambition is to get Sámi voices to be heard and understood at the national level. We have consultations on industrial development, but the ministries' policy and

---

134 *61/295. United Nations Declaration on the Rights of Indigenous Peoples* (New York: United Nations, 2008).

135 Johnsen, Mathiesen, and Gaup Eira, "Sami reindeer governance in Norway."

decisions don't reflect our voices. I want to help younger people build the capacity and get the education to talk to politicians, on an international level too. The national government's perception about our rights must change."

In what are known to be some of the most equitable, successful countries in the world—Norway, Finland, Sweden—Indigenous people are living without the right to self-determination of their lands and livelihoods. Just add that to the list of things they never taught us at university.

In all my years in Alaska, in addition to my formal education, I primarily learned how to view the world with a western mindset. I wouldn't have the skills or the hands-on experience to steward the land from a reindeer herders' perspective. I would contend that the same is true for the majority of environmental scientists and professionals. It is important that we recognize the value of *árbediehtu* and other Indigenous knowledge systems. Environmental departments and organizations should be looking to institutionalize better power-sharing mechanisms with Sámi for management of reindeer herding lands. Not only for the good of the environment, but also to continue building the Sámi culture and developing *árbediehtu* for future generations—as international law requires the government to do.

CHAPTER 12

GREEN COLONIALISM

———

It is time we put an end to the epistemic silences in
predominant climate change discourses, which erase and
ignore the agency, knowledge, and experiences of non-
Western, non-White peoples, and Indigenous communities.
—JAMES THUO GATHII

When the herders finished tagging and assessing their reindeer for the day, it was time to move them from the smaller
corral into a larger fenced area. A type of sliding door was
anchored into the mud between the corral and larger area,
and I hopped up to help untie the ropes holding it in place.
All the while, the gigantic herd continued swirling around,
many large eyes flicking toward us as we messed with the
fence. Others hoisted the posts of the door out of the mud
and ran to the side as the herd began to stampede through
the new opening.

Like water poured from a vase, the round, muscular animals hurtled down the mountainside to disperse themselves
freely along the tundra. There were so many reindeer, it took
minutes for them to push through the opening ten at a time,

side by side. During the procession, my ears filled with the stamping of hooves and howling wind over the hillside. A few reindeer wore bells that chimed as they ran, and others called out to their babies in ungulate grunts, *Ow ow, ow ow.*

When it ended, a few people hitched up their four-wheelers to drive down the hill and eat dinner at the cabin. Ole-Ante and I, as well as a few others, trekked down the squishy tundra in our waterproof boots. The sun was covered over with gray clouds, and snow began to dust the higher elevations above us. In Anchorage we called that "termination dust"—the first snow on the mountains meant that full-on winter was soon to come below. For now, the lower tundra remained a vibrant mix of blueberry leaves turned to a signature autumnal red, fluffy white reindeer lichen, and green mosses. As we walked over it, our view was the expanse of blue ocean ahead.

"What is your ideal job?" I asked Ole-Ante. I was in mine. I loved that working with environmental policy allowed me to be outdoors like this, if only rarely. I also adored the opportunity to learn from people who grew up differently than me; it seemed like the only way to learn.

Ole-Ante said, "In an ideal world, I would be a reindeer herder with more freedoms. But it's not happening, and industrial development is a big driver."

During the time I lived in Sápmi, the Norwegian government approved multiple contentious projects on reindeer-herding lands. There was the Arctic Railway, for which plans cut directly through undeveloped reindeer husbandry areas to connect the Arctic Ocean to Europe, without formal opportunity for Sámi to participate in planning.[136] The gov-

---

136 Thomas Nilsen, "The dream of an Arctic railway fades as Sami herders signal 'veto,'" *ArcticToday*, March 5, 2020.

ernment also approved a new copper mine at Hammerfest that would dump metal-heavy tailings directly into fjord waters; the government directly declined Sámi people's appeals, causing a protest of more than 4,500 people without formal participation.[137] During my final month in Norway, the government cleared the largest-ever wind farm to be built on Sámi lands.[138]

These projects fell into an historical pattern. An event called "the Alta Controversy" inspired the Sámi movement. Back in 1970, a Norwegian government administration announced plans to dam the Alta River to provide hydroelectricity in the North. The dam would flood a huge reindeer herding area that included the Sámi town of Masi. The government cleared procedural hurdles without ever including Sámi and began construction on the dam in 1979. Multiple protests including Sámi and Norwegians took place: protesters chained themselves to a barrier onsite to stop construction, while others led a hunger strike in Oslo to petition the project. From the national government to the Supreme Court of Norway, multiple government decisions denied Sámi rights to the land; one-tenth of the Norwegian police force was finally called in to remove protesters. The Norwegian government ultimately flooded the land, and the dam began producing electricity in 1987.[139]

Back then and today, the protests inspired young Sámi to fight for their rights. As we walked back down the tundra,

137 Thomas Nilsen, "Norway greenlights copper mine with tailings to be dumped in Arctic fjord," *The Barents Observer*, November 30, 2019.

138 Kevin McGwin, "Reindeer herders say they will sue to halt Norway's largest wind farm," *ArcticToday*, July 1, 2020.

139 William Lawrence, "Saami and Norwegians protest construction of Alta Dam, Norway, 1979-1981," Global Nonviolent Action Database, January 30, 2011.

Ole-Ante told me about his reasons for educating about Sámi rights.

"Here's a story," he said. "Sámi children have very different upbringings from western children."

Ole-Ante was the oldest of three boys. Sámi children, he explained, are encouraged to handle much more responsibility from a younger age. Ole-Ante grew up around reindeer and the north Sámi language from the time he was born. His father, Hamni, was a well-known reindeer herder in a town called Guovdageaidnu on the Norwegian side of Sápmi, where the local high school focused on education in reindeer husbandry. The majority of children were expected to know how to use a knife to slice meat, as well as build and tend to a fire.

Like his ancestors before him, Ole-Ante spent the first years of his life following his family's herd from pasture to pasture on the tundra, fall to spring. One December when he was seven or eight, Ole-Ante's dad packed him, his two brothers, and a *lavvu* for sleeping on the back of his snow machine for a multi-night trip to check the herds. The sun would never rise above the horizon on their trip, so they also packed a lamp.

After hours of driving over forty miles per hour on the open tundra, his dad's snow machine broke down. They tinkered with it as much as possible, but it was dead. Before snow machines, Sámi used skis and sleds to traverse the ice and snow. Now the only pair Ole-Ante's dad had with him were his son's tiny set, but they would have to do. Ole-Ante's dad helped the children set up the *lavvu*, then took off on tiny red skis after the herd.

"A reindeer herder can't fail," Ole-Ante said. "Failure leads to death."

Ole-Ante wished he could gain even 50 percent of the abilities and skills of his father, Hamni. Hamni was a revered knowledge-holder in the community. If anyone was unsure about why their reindeer was sick, which should be slaughtered, or how to properly take care of them in the unpredictable weather, he was the expert they asked for advice. Hamni had to keep moving to protect the entire family's livelihood from scattering across the tundra, becoming prey, starving, and inter-mixing with other herders' animals. Imagine if the majority of your entire family's investment and income could run off on four legs into a wilderness the size of Maryland.

As freezing winds howled around their *lavvu*, Ole-Ante, his year-younger brother, and their four-year-old baby sibling waited for their father for three days. While his brothers slept on the reindeer hides laid around the snowy *lavvu* floor, he fed a fire in the center with shrubs from the *duottar*, the tundra. When the antsy boys cried to go watch the aurora in the bitter cold, he told them it was best to hide from a big bull moose outside. As the eldest, he was used to the responsibility. Just as his dad had to watch the reindeer at all costs, this experience inspired Ole-Ante to pay diligent attention to his family's needs.

On the third day a local politician on his snowmobile pulled up to the lonely *lavvu* to say hello and found the children inside. Everyone in town knew each other, and certainly knew the Turi family. Ole-Ante remembers the politician pulling a brick-sized, antennae cell phone from his front pouch to call Uncle Johan Mathis, the man I sat with at the fire.

As one of the founders of the Association of World Reindeer Herders, Johan Mathis was a lifelong advocate for international collaboration among reindeer herders of all ethnicities. He argued that, from Sápmi to the North and Far East of Russia, reindeer herding had enabled the sustainable use of resources like lichen and fungi that would otherwise go unused by people. The resulting lifeways and culture sustained communities of Sámi, Dolgans, Yukagir, Evenki, Nenets, and many more peoples for as long as can be remembered.[140] Even though it was a hard life, it had allowed people and reindeer to thrive in a biodiverse Arctic for millennia. Ole-Ante strived to continue the legacy of his uncle and ancestors before him.

"Things are difficult for the reindeer herders," Ole-Ante concluded. "Experiences like that remind you that you are hardy. If you could cope with something like that as a child, you can cope with whatever comes."

Ole-Ante was talking about resilience. The reindeer herding lifestyle was not for everyone; that was true. There was the weather to consider, made more difficult by climate change. There were the government's assimilative policies, which wreak havoc on your identity and livelihood. I don't think we'll be able to solve the world's most difficult challenges like climate change and institutionalized inequity until we center the people at the front lines in decision-making. They are the ones who encountered these challenges firsthand and can identify the systemic changes needed to solve them.

At an Arctic conference, an elder once asked me to write down my story. He wanted me to publish the steps I took to get into Arctic policy administration, so other northern youth could seek those opportunities. For too many of us, government decision-making seems impossibly far out of reach. What I found is that the table where decisions are made

---

140 Johan Mathis Turi, "Native reindeer herders' priorities for research," *Polar Research* 19, no. 1 (2000): 131-133.

is quite exclusionary, and code-switching is an unspoken job requirement. We still need more Black and Indigenous people operating from their own worldviews in policy administration if we want decision-makers to be receptive to political change.

In high school, the first job I applied to was a summer internship with one of Alaska's two senators. I poured my heart into a cover letter about my perspectives on racism in Alaska, the difficult experience of my dad passing away, and how it had inspired me to make Alaska a better, more inclusive place. Looking back, perhaps I shared too much; I should have been more politically savvy and understood my audience. But I knew then, and I continue to believe now, that the most truthful story from your heart is the one people need to hear. Most people will feel grateful and empowered by honesty.

Well, the senator never responded to my application. When I read through the cohort of interns, I only recognized a wealthy girl from my school whose grandfather had been a prominent Alaska politician. It figures.

My first real breakthrough into the policy world occurred when I studied abroad. The cost of the study abroad program covered our registration fees to an Arctic conference gathering thousands of business, political, and scientific leaders. Over the course of the week, dozens of concurrent panels ran from eight in the morning to eight at night. I carried my pen and pad from room to room, diligently taking notes. I had written blogs in an internship the summer before and proposed to my previous employer to write a blog about my experiences at the conference.[141]

---

141 Michaela Stith, "Big ships welcomed at the Arctic Circle conference," *Friends of the Earth* (blog), Medium, December 22, 2016.

(This is advice for all young people who want to go far: Jump on any opportunity that is given to you and make something bigger of it. Always ask for more, and always ask twice.)

I learned a great deal; not only was the Arctic Ocean becoming ice-free, but everyone from scientists to cargo ship operators to energy industry representatives from Maine to China and back wanted a piece of this new real estate. Many saw the melting of the Arctic not as a disastrous shift in peoples' ways of life, but as an economic opportunity in a sparsely populated place. Given that the vast majority of people above Alaska's Arctic Circle are Indigenous, I expected the panels to be somewhat representative. Yet from one session to the next, I noticed a pattern of whiteness.

The conference goers seemed to be making decisions for people they'd never met in places they'd never been. Or they'd been there a couple times and were now considered experts. Meanwhile, the real experts were at home. I felt all over again what I felt back in my Highly Gifted classes: These people do not represent home. They do not know Arctic people or much about the place they come from. Why are they the leaders of our future?

Reflecting on my own opportunities, the answer is usually money and networks. Capital and capitalist friends. I was able to attend that conference because my study abroad program arranged it, and my university paid for it. I was able to enroll in a wealthy university because I attended one of, if not the most, exclusive educational program in the state of Alaska. I spent my afternoons and weekends at high school debate tournaments, work, and other extracurricular activities. In Alaska, only 77 percent of students graduate from high school, and a quarter of the people who start college in the state finish in six years.[142,143] The closer I got to powerful people, the more my experiences diverged from people with whom I grew up. If I was going to be in this type of arena, I wanted to be a voice to amplify what I heard at home.

When Ole-Ante graduated high school, Norwegian state restrictions on herding meant individuals in the *siida* would not be allowed to continue herding. In the reindeer husbandry acts of the 1970s, Norwegians created assimilative policies to "modernize" traditional Sámi reindeer herding and increase meat production. The new acts provided subsidies and incentives to build permanent enclosures, buy vehicles, and generally capitalize reindeer meat production as an industry.[144] The government also gave incentives to herders who stimulated a higher ratio of female deer, in order to increase herd sizes.[145] But now that their policies have resulted in more deer, the reindeer herding administration says the number and weight of reindeer per area is unsustainable, according to their own scientific models. They limited the number of reindeer herders to reduce "overgrazing" of pasture lands.

It seems to me that the Norwegian government created the problem of overgrazing. It has always sought control over reindeer herding in some form or another—regardless of what little specified knowledge scientists had on the subject.

Over time, the government restrictions changed Ole-Ante's dream job. He agreed with his family to leave the *siida*

---

142 "Top Graduation Rate Public Schools in Alaska," Public School Review, accessed March 5, 2021.

143 Andy Kiersz, "The 15 US states with the lowest college graduation rates," *Business Insider*, June 7, 2019.

144 Johnsen, Mathiesen, and Gaup Eira, "Sami reindeer governance in Norway."

145 Ibid.

for a few years and began to train in the military upon graduation. Some of his proudest achievements came from that time, and he was able to save many lives. Ole-Ante— called Ole-Anders among the Norwegian ranks—leveraged the grit and stamina earned in the *duottar*. Soon after the military, he enrolled at UiT, The Arctic University of Norway in Tromsø, to study political science. If the government was going to make policies that affected Sámi people, Ole-Ante wanted to be part of making them as harmless and beneficial as possible.

In the seven years after high school, Ole-Ante lost the opportunity to learn *árbediehtu*, Sámi knowledge, that his brothers had. Though he is oldest, the middle brother is now the most skilled of them. Sadly, Hamni passed away before Ole-Ante had the chance to return to reindeer husbandry. Were it not for modern-day green colonialism, the choice between his culture and chosen livelihood wouldn't be necessary; as a reindeer herder, they would have been one and the same.

Today Ole-Ante is an advisor with the Sámi Parliament. He uses his time outside and inside work to reconnect with reindeer herding. He still struggles to have time for two full-time jobs: advising the Parliament on Sámi society, culture, and health related to reindeer husbandry, as well as spending time on the land as a reindeer herder himself. He committed that time regardless because the job allowed him freedom to shape and solve the challenges posed by climate change, the loss of pasture and grazing land, and national ambitions to Norwegianize reindeer herding.

This is the root of the problem: White people have annexed Indigenous lands, stolen Black people away from theirs, and otherwise gained control of resources all around the world, where the people who live there now live disproportionately in poverty. As a result, we must enter these white institutions for access to our own self-governance.

The opportunities that allowed Ole-Ante and me to interlope with policy making are also culturally discordant for many folks in the Arctic. Students who speak Indigenous languages rarely have the opportunity to use them in school, and they become immersed in courses based on western paradigms. Governments across the Arctic have scantily invested in northern institutions of higher education. This means most Arctic Indigenous students must travel south to receive a degree from historically white institutions.[146] The discrimination and policies imposed on our communities pressure northerners even more to move away or adopt western lifestyles.

"One of the biggest challenges in reindeer herding," Ole-Ante said as we continued walking down the hill at Reinøya, "is modern-day loss of pasture lands for wind farms, hydro dams, and mining."

In contrast to the administration's view that reindeer herding is unsustainable, reindeer herders themselves say that industrial growth is the largest factor of land degradation in northern Norway.[147] While reindeer herders work with pastures and keep them relatively wild, the government continues to dispossess these lands to build sites of renewable

146 Arctic Council Indigenous Peoples' Secretariat, *Permanent Participant Panel at the UArctic Congress, September 2018 "Education and training in the Arctic: Identifying education and training needs for Arctic Indigenous Peoples"* (Tromsø: Arctic Council Open Access Archive, 2018).

147 Kathrine Ivsett Johnsen, "Conflicting knowledges, competing worldviews: Norwegian governance of Sámi reindeer husbandry in West Finnmark, Norway" (doctoral thesis, Norwegian University of Life Sciences, Ås, 2018).

and extractive industrial activity—and has the gall to call reindeer husbandry "unsustainable" at the same time.[148]

"Why are wind farms a problem?" I asked. Before coming to Norway, I was amazed that the country quadrupled its number of wind turbines in the past ten years, and many of the onshore projects were built in the wide-open lands of the North.[149] As someone trained in environmental science and policy, Norway's progress on energy transition seemed laudable. I'd often lamented the minimal renewable energy projects in Alaska, despite our excess of geothermal, wind, and hydro energy sources.

"Reindeer stay away from the sound of the turbines," Ole-Ante answered.

He gestured toward the wide-open scene around us: there wasn't a building in sight. From the hillside of Reinøya, we could see clear across the blue fjord to the snow-topped ridges of Finnmark in the north. The only sound were our own voices, the wind ruffling by our ears, and distant "ow ows" where reindeer grazed.

Even though reindeer migration routes and wind turbines can coexist on paper, turbines in reindeer pastures effectively reduce the extent of pasture lands. In addition to sound, turbines bring new roads and buildings. Renewable energy infrastructure also requires increased mining for critical minerals, which often takes place in reindeer herding lands. All these activities reduce pasture lands where there was previously no industrial development.

---

148 Kathrine Ivsett Johnsen, "The paradox of reindeer pasture management in Finnmark, Norway," Strategic Environmental Impact Assessment of Development of the Arctic, September 2014.

149 Weronika Strzyżyńska, "Sámi reindeer herders file lawsuit against Norway windfarm," *The Guardian*, January 18, 2021._

It's ironic that efforts to reduce carbon emissions to fight climate change have impacted people who lead the most sustainable, traditional livelihoods. That's because climate change is a cultural problem embedded in our relationship with the environment. A "green economy" dependent on renewable energy is not fundamentally different from economic models of the past. Even when replacing fossil fuels with hydropower and wind energy, valleys must be flooded, land cleared, and new roads built to maintain those new energy sources. You also need more mined metals to build windmills, solar panels, and vehicle batteries, which may conflict with traditional economies.[150] As long as the government needs energy to fuel a growth-based economy, it will always require cheap land and resources, which often come at the expense of the people who live on and around them.

To isolate itself from criticism while transitioning to a green economy, the Norwegian government has historically excluded Sámi from the decision-making process.[151] This process is what the Sámi have called "green colonialism." The lands lost to one wind farm can eliminate the possibility of reindeer herding for an entire *siida*.[152] Industrial projects like wind farms manifest not only income loss for the family, but also loss of the knowledge that makes up Sámi culture among reindeer herders. Yet Sámi are not meaningfully included in the planning processes for new development.

---

150 Thomas Nilsen, "How miners' hunt for metals to power electric cars threatens Sámi reindeer herders' homeland," *ArcticToday*, July 13, 2020.

151 Chad M. Briggs, "Science, local knowledge and exclusionary practices: Lessons from the Alta Dam case," *Norsk Geografisk Tidsskrift— Norwegian Journal of Geography* 60, no. 2 (2006), 149-160.

152 Strzyżyńska, "Sámi reindeer herders file lawsuit against Norway windfarm."

"Sámi are not opposed to economic development," Ole-Ante clarified, hands touching the lasso around his chest. "But a reindeer herder will receive one call asking their opinion of a development project, say the project sounds interesting, and suddenly the project has approval. We learn to say 'no' to developers, unless our positive attitudes end up resulting in loss of the pasture lands."

The alternative to green colonialism is to include Sámi at all levels of decision-making for industrial developments in their homelands, including early planning stages. In fact, climate change efforts should focus on human rights. Since Sámi are rightsholders—not only stakeholders—to their pasture areas, they deserve the final say on development projects. It is crucial for decision makers to understand that acceptance from reindeer herders is required before building begins. Enter Ole-Ante: Due to the resilience he learned as a child, he's come up with a new dream job.

"The learned skills among the Sámi reindeer herders' youth can enable them to create and keep a dialogue between decision-making organs and *siidas*," said Ole-Ante. One day, he would like to use his mixed knowledge of political science and *árbediehtu* to keep dialogue between government, industry, and reindeer herders.

I think this is the future of decision-making. Young people from all different backgrounds now have college degrees, even if they had to sacrifice much more to earn them than people who inherited a western world view, wealth, and white privilege. We possess the knowledge and requirements to sit around the table, but decision-makers have not yet recognized the value of non-western world views. They still walk into a conference full of western, white people and think, "This is okay." *That* is one of the first cultural shifts western societies need to make.

No matter how Black and Indigenous peoples may think differently than the status quo in government, we matter. We deserve to be part of the process in making decisions that affect us.

CHAPTER 13

TUTTU

We have often heard people within academia, policy and management speak to us of nutritional value, calories and money needed to purchase food. All of this is important, but not what we are talking about when we say food security.

—INUIT CIRCUMPOLAR COUNCIL

I straddled a roaring snow machine and grasped my arms around the driver in front of me: Eben, an Arctic Youth Ambassador visiting Guovdageaidnu from the North Slope of Alaska. Tuomma, the same from Reinøya, led the two of us and four other Ambassadors on a team of snow machines over frozen lakes toward his herd. The students I traveled with had flown to Sápmi from all over Alaska, from the southeast and the Aleutian Islands. The Arctic Youth Ambassadors program elected teenage students to travel in the USA and abroad to bring awareness about life in Alaska. In Sápmi, I met other Alaskans with deeply personal reasons for educating others about the drastic effects of climate change.

Like a metro in the city, thick ice is essential for safe travel in communities around the circumpolar Arctic.[153] Where there are no connecting roads between people and their food, people travel by sled dogs and snow machines to traverse lakes, mountains, bays, and marshes. Ice used to reign around the Arctic Ocean eight months of the year near the 1970s, but now Arctic ice is much less reliable than a subway timetable.

It was early January, and the sun hadn't shown itself this far north for the last two months. The dim winter light shone blue on the snow as far as the eye could see, with only twisted, slender trees standing above the *duottar*, tundra. Helmets protected us from the wind; parkas, pants, and boots shielded from the cold. It was minus sixteen degrees Celsius out. I wore a wool sweater, long johns, chunky knit stockings, two pairs of thick socks, snowsuit overalls, and a heavy coat, with a black face mask that covered everywhere but my eyes. I was so bundled in layers that I didn't have a full range of motion.

I had Ski-Dooed donuts on frozen lakes a handful of times on New Year's, but I had never had a snow machine of my own. I did not usually do outdoor activities in the winter before college; I spent hours after school every day at debate practice. As my mom liked to tell her family in Tennessee, our life was not like Sarah Palin's Alaska.

In eighteen-year-old Eben Hopson's Alaska, a snow machine was crucial for food security. Like his Iñupiaq ancestors before him, Eben provided food for many families in his community by hunting caribou, whaling twice a year, and fishing in the summer. Whenever Eben was not working or at

---

153 Arctic Research Consortium of the United States, "Arctic Futures 2050 Conference: Day 2," September 5, 2015, video, 12:13-14:24, featuring Maija Lukin.

school, he was either actively hunting or prepping equipment. Hunting required hours at a time spent on the land; every morning he woke up early to go outside, check the weather, and plan his day based on how the sky, wind, and temperature felt. A new snow machine to traverse the land would be too expensive, but he saved up over months to buy a used one and used his experiential knowledge in mechanics to keep it running. I felt safe with Eben driving.

Face pressed against his weatherproof back, I absorbed the Arctic scene zooming past and the indigo blue sky above us. A smile bloomed under my mask as I imagined how green and purple aurora—*Kiuġuyat* in Iñupiaq—would light up around the moon at night.[154] The cold blasting into my body and the scenery before my eyes made me feel giddy. Nothing could be heard over the deafening sounds of the machine underneath us and wind howling past our ears. For at least twenty minutes of our drive, I belted my best Alicia Keys impression into the back of Eben's head. Then I tried to remember as many words as I could to Drake's "Nonstop." Eben kept his focus on the trail and thumb on the throttle, unaware of my personal concert.

Suddenly the Ski-Doo nose-dived from a steep bank onto a semi-frozen lake. The song drained from my lungs as my stomach lurched toward my mouth. My jaw clenched and I held on tight as the snow machine bucked over the liquid snowy bank. Eben let off the throttle for a moment, and the two skis at the front floundered under an inch of water.

Up ahead, we could see the other ambassadors were safely crossing, spraying trails of water behind them. Eben regained

---

154 "Kiuguyat: The Northern Lights," University of Alaska Anchorage, accessed March 22, 2021.

his nerve and leaned over the handles as he fed the snow machine gas. The snow machine track whirred as its gears ground into the slush. The key to crossing successfully was never slowing down—if Eben did, the thin lake ice might crack and engulf us in freezing water.

At sixteen degrees below zero Celsius, it was warmer in January than Eben was used to. At home in Utqiaġvik, the northernmost town in North America, winter dipped to negative fifty without wind chill. The sea ice on the North Slope froze the ocean up to the shore in late December, and only reached slushy temperatures during spring break-up season. But, with a football field's worth of ice shrinking from the Arctic each month, traveling over ice had become increasingly dangerous. Snow machines were known to fall through the open water between cracks in the ice. Underwater, it would only take three minutes to die from hypothermia.

Within those few terrifying moments, the machine gained traction again and zoomed over the lake. Once we made it across, we paused a few moments to calm.

"Are you okay?" he turned his head to ask, remaining seated on the machine.

"I'm okay!" I said. "I trust your driving. Are you okay?"

He was quiet for a moment. "The last time I drove a snow machine, I had a really bad accident."

Just a few months before, the ice suddenly gave way beneath him. It was terrifying, because every Inuk knows someone who has fallen through the ice and died.[155] Many of those people were experienced, lifelong hunters. Yet recent ice loss made travel unsafe in traditional and familial hunting

---

155 Terry Hansen, "More People Are Falling Through the Arctic's Melting Ice Never to Be Seen Again," *Motherboard: Tech by Vice* (blog), Vice Media Group, September 16, 2019.

areas. In the last two generations, over 70 percent of sea ice on the Arctic Ocean rapidly disappeared.[156] Over two hundred Alaskans died from falling through the ice from 1990–2010, with Indigenous people passing away at more than four times the rate of all Alaskans.[157]

The reason for the discrepancy was that Alaska Native people traveled on the land more frequently and at longer distances in order to provide food.[158] For a subsistence hunter, it was crucial to bring back sustenance for the community. Eben shook out his arms and took a deep breath.

"Something I heard," he said. "No matter what happens, never stop going out on the land."

Despite the risks to traversing the melting icy landscape, it was important to him to practice and preserve the culture. After all, his grandfather's name, Eben Hopson, decorated his local middle school in big, bold letters. Eben's grand-father was the very first mayor of Barrow, now called its Iñupiaq name, Utqiaġvik. He was also the founder of the Inuit Circumpolar Conference—the largest and oldest repre-sentative body of Inuit people across Russia, Alaska, Canada, and Greenland.[159] Today, ICC represents over 180,000 Inuit across the Arctic in fora like the United Nations and the Arctic Council.[160]

---

156 Arctic Research Consortium of the United States, "After the Ice - Part 1: Our Food," October 7, 2020, video, 7:34.

157 N.L. Fleischer et al., "The epidemiology of falling-through-the-ice in Alaska, 1990–2010," *Journal of Public Health* 36, no. 2 (June 2014): 235–242.

158 Ibid.

159 "A Short Biography on the Honorable Eben Hopson," Eben Hopson Memorial Archives, accessed February 6, 2021.

160 "About ICC," Inuit Circumpolar Council, accessed February 7, 2021.

"I feel like carrying his name is a big deal because he did important things for our people during his time. I need to do something for our people now," Eben said.

Hearing about his grandfather's history-making achievements as a child sparked Eben's interest in speaking up about the harsh truths and realities of life in the high Arctic. He began his own film company, Driftwood Productions, to share videos and images of working on the land. He endeavored to change the narratives about the Arctic dominated by non-Arctic points of view.

Eben and his family had a great deal of knowledge to share. Archaeological evidence shows that Inuit have been hunting whales and seals in Eben's region for at least 13,800 years. That is an order of magnitude longer than the Stonehenge, Colosseum, Pyramids of Giza, and Easter Island statues have been on Earth, and two orders longer than the Great Wall of China.[161]

Eben had never traveled abroad before this trip and had been anxious about traveling so far from Alaska. But when he got out to the tundra, it felt like the Arctic. Like home.

The purpose of the Arctic Youth Ambassadors' exchange was to expose the Alaskans traveling abroad to the challenges reindeer herders face due to climate change. The takeaway was a positive one, though: Indigenous knowledge is a powerful tool in adapting to climate change. We rumbled over lakes and tundra for another hour through the night-day before Tuomma pushed on his brakes and raised his deer-hide mitten in the freezing air.

The five of our snowmobiles powered down at the edge of the clearing. Too much noise would scare his herd off,

---

161 Arctic Research Consortium of the United States, "12 - Melting Ice & Thawing Permafrost," panel at Arctic Futures 2050, September 23, 2019, video, 9:00-11:45, featuring Maija Lukin.

Tuomma said. He silently pointed toward a few black specks beyond a snowy drift. By now it was afternoon, and the stars began to shine through the navy-indigo ceiling. The snow reflected all the light it found and showed up a dusty blue, darkened by the shadows of child-sized shrubs. When my eyes adjusted, I saw reindeer kneeling their snouts into the snow. Somewhere in the distant back of the field, a few hundred reindeer munched for food. I narrowed my eyes to focus in on the herd, but ice shone off the ends of my eyelashes and almost blocked my view.

"The harsh cold inland is better for grazing," Tuomma told us.

Tuomma typically used few words, unless he had a joke to tell. If it wasn't sixteen below, he probably would have been rolling a cigarette with bare fingers. Since I had last seen him, Tuomma had herded his reindeer five hundred kilometers north from Reinøya. His family would have led them on foot or sled in the past, but Norwegian urbanization along the traditional path made that impossible. Beginning every December, Tuomma loaded his *siida*'s thousands of deer onto cargo shipping trucks and drove them north along the highway. It was mid-January now, and the reindeer had been grazing in northwestern Finnmark for a month.

Here were just a few. While we waited for the reindeer to come to us, he started to kick a hole in the snow with his foot. Tuomma motioned and we crowded around.

"Come look," Tuomma said. "There are layers in the snow."

Tuomma reached in the hole and shook a layer of snow, packed in soft and powdery. This was "good grazing," Tuomma told us; the type of snow reindeer could munch through. Reindeer have to eat all year round, of course, even in winter. Their tough snouts dug down into the snow to get at frozen lichen and other freezer-section treats. The reindeer herders' job was to lead them toward such accommodating snow patches.

He then cracked a layer of crunchy, crystalline snow off the top of the blanket and said, "We call this sugar snow in *Sámigiella*." Using his mother tongue, Tuomma drew out each syllable of the word like molasses. Sugar snow, he explained, came from rainfall in winter. When rain turned existing snow turned to crystalline ice, it created a hard layer. The reindeers' snouts couldn't penetrate it.

"This is why good grazing is important," Tuomma continued. "Good grazing" means food is accessible. When ice forms a layer over the snow, reindeer can't access the frozen lichen. Along the coast, like in Tromsø, rains occurred all winter long. Inland, the temperatures stayed below zero degrees Celsius during the winter and left less possibility for rain. Unfortunately, warmer temperatures are leading to more rain-on-snow events in Arctic winter. Ice formation from rain-on-snow events—sugar snow—is associated with catastrophic mass starvation of reindeer herds.[162] These reindeer were in the heart of winter pastures, where they could normally dig through the dry snow and snack on frozen lichen all winter long. Rain had been here recently and that wasn't normal.

The Intergovernmental Panel on Climate Change (IPCC) says, "restrictions affecting the movement of reindeer to pastures are expected to negatively interact with the effects of climate and affect the future sustainability of herding systems" across the Arctic region.[163] Essentially, climate change is mak-

---

162 Kevin McGwin, "Sámi herders fear supplementary feeding is changing the nature of their livelihood," *ArcticToday*, February 11, 2021.

163 Intergovernmental Panel on Climate Change (IPCC), "Special Report on the Ocean and Cryosphere in a Changing Climate (SROCC): Chapter 3, Polar Regions," accessed March 24, 2021.

ing reindeer herding harder, but government policies and land conflicts set up many of the barriers to adaptation. In the past, reindeer herders could lead their herds to better grazing areas. But northern Norway has become more industrialized, and personal implementation plans limit the locations where herds can legally graze. Some families less fortunate than Tuomma used to utilize winter pastures in Finland and can no longer herd there legally because of border restrictions.

Now, herders lay food pellets on the ground when they can't access good grazing and pastures.[164] Food pellets were not the traditional way; since reindeer traditionally fed on local foliage, feeding food pellets was less sustainable and resulted in different quality meat. That really hurt, because ensuring high quality meat meant everything to a serious herder like Tuomma.

Eben's livelihood was also affected by climate change. In addition to dangerous cracks and open water, the loss of year-round sea ice has caused major storms to wrack the coastline. Back in the 1970s, high winds and strong ocean currents pushed thick ice sheets together to form towering *ivuniq*—similar to the way magma pushes tectonic plates together to form mountains. These icy pressure ridges used to be three or four stories tall and blocked the coast from storms.[165] In the last few years, ten- to fifteen-foot waves flooded beaches around Eben's town.[166] The two major roads

164 Malia Wollan, "How to Herd Reindeer," *New York Times*, February 11, 2020.

165 Northern Alaska Sea Ice Project Jukebox, "Roy and Savik Ahmaogak, Part 1," Digital Branch of the University of Alaska Fairbanks Oral History Program, June 1, 2017.

166 "10-15 Foot Waves Break Seawall at Barrow, Alaska," *Robertscribbler* (blog), Dark Forest Press, August 27, 2015.

he used to haul his fishing and hunting equipment from late spring to early fall are now wiped away; one is completely underwater. Without access to the best spots, fishing and hunting would be poor this coming season.

"Does that impact people's ability to eat?" I asked. I recalled that grocery store milk was eight dollars a gallon because of exorbitant shipping costs to reach the North Slope, and most rural Alaskan households relied on subsistence.

"Yes, definitely," Eben told me. "Our food security depends on traditionally sourced foods."

Iñupiaq have traditionally stored their catch in an underground ice cellar, called *sigluaq*, making use of year-round permafrost. Eben said he notices more rainfall every year. In the early summer, relentless rain floods the underground cellars and thaws the permafrost as well as the food. Bowhead whale intended to feed a family through the winter would be lost, and there would be seven months of winter before the community could renew their seasonal quota.

Since 1979, the Alaska Eskimo Whaling Commission has been tasked with proving how many whales can be sustainably caught.[167] Even today, seasonal quotas are established with data from *Qallunaaq*, primarily white outsiders, who fly in to counter the Iñupiaq data with anthropological assessments. Like Tuomma's herding, Eben's whaling was made even more difficult by government restrictions. The world's inaction on climate change, compounded by government regulations, has resulted in tangible losses for Arctic providers.

Meanwhile, high carbon dioxide emitters pay nothing to compensate for their externalities. "Externality" is an economic term that describes side effects caused by producing

167 "People of the Ice Whale," Peak Three, video, 9:44.

or consuming a good which impact third parties not directly related to the transaction.[168] For example, neither the passengers, the airline, nor the fueling company are required to pay for the carbon dioxide emissions caused by a long-haul flight, but Arctic residents' food security is threatened nonetheless. People with the smallest carbon footprints—who produce their sustenance from the land around them—are the most impacted by climate change.

A lot of people subsequently assume that climate change will be the demise of Arctic Indigenous peoples.[169] But that is not what I took away from spending time with people who herd reindeer or lead subsistence lifestyles. I noticed how much specific knowledge they have about the Arctic environment, down to very small differences in snow texture. Even the IPCC says "[t]he tightly coupled relationship of northern local communities and their environment provide an opportunity to better understand climate change and its effects, support adaptation, and limit unintended consequences."[170] The world has a lot to learn from Indigenous peoples about the impacts of climate change, as well as ways to mitigate carbon emissions. In the Amazon rainforest, for example, Indigenous territories reduced deforestation twice as fast as government-protected nature areas.[171] Indigenous

168 Tejvan Pettinger, "Externalities—definition," *Economics Help* (blog), accessed March 7, 2021.

169 Andrew Stuhl, *Unfreezing the Arctic: Science, Colonialism, and the Transformation of Inuit Lands* (Chicago: University of Chicago Press, 2016), chap. 5.

170 IPCC, *Special Report on the Ocean and Cryosphere in a Changing Climate*.

171 FAO and FILAC, *Forest governance by indigenous and tribal peoples. An opportunity for climate action in Latin America and the Caribbean* (Santiago: FAO, 2021).

peoples' control over their own lands is important for our planet's future.

As we climbed back onto the snow machines, Tuomma led us toward his cabin for dinner. We disappeared into a cloud of snow until pulling up at the small wooden beacon in the endless expanse of frozen hills. The sky above it cascaded above us like a star-speckled dome, amplified bright with the snow's reflection of moonshine. The three-room cabin was equipped with a TV and a large antenna on the roof, a running sink and kitchen, and an outhouse latrine in the front yard. I stomped through the snow heaps to regain feeling in my toes, unlatched the round snowmobile helmet, peeled off the parka, threw the heavy boots and snow pants to the side. My phone had died from the sheer cold. While it charged and Tuomma cooked, the Arctic Youth Ambassadors and I patiently sat around the cabin's dining room table in our base layers.

"Norwegians say the best way to have meat is tenderloin fried in a pan, but what do they know?" Tuomma declared while he stirred a pot full of water, reindeer, and a bit of salt. "Sámi have been eating reindeer for millennia. Why shouldn't we be the judge?"

My new friends from Alaska got excited as the smell wafted from the kitchen to our noses. Most people they knew preferred country foods over store-bought meat.

"I would choose our native foods any day of the year," Eben said, in between spoonfuls. "It's healthier and higher-quality meat, you know where it comes from, and it's not so expensive. Sometimes I've treated myself to a steak for eight dollars a pound from the store, but it's not as filling. Not when I can get a 150-pound male caribou for $2.50—the cost of my bullet."

Though reindeer were less common in Utqiaġvik, Eben was used to caribou. The wild cousins migrated annually across Canada and Alaska. When he saw *tuttu* on the horizon,

Eben would hunt for them by himself or with a group of cousins. Then, he would distribute the meat to families who relied on his hunting skills.

Tuomma ladled our stew into bowls and brought them to the table. It was made from the best part of reindeer, according to Tuomma: the spine. The broth was flavorful and rich, meaty like you would expect, but lean and fresh tasting.

"It tastes like *tuttu*," said Eben, grinning between spoonfuls. "Just like home."

Home is where the heart is, and Eben's heart was in the Arctic. Though Sápmi and Alaska were located on different continents, people around the circumpolar North shared some similar experiences. Up in the North, people speak at a protracted pace. Some ride snow machines across the tundra to provide for their relatives, be they Sámi or Iñupiaq.

Just like the residential schools in Sápmi, Alaska Native children were sent to boarding schools in Sitka and Bethel, Alaska, or as far away as Oregon and Oklahoma for Christian-run, state-sanctioned education.[172] Iñupiaq and other Alaska Native youth were taught their languages and ways of life were backward and unworthy of discussion. School staff sexually assaulted and physically and mentally abused children. Many returned to the Arctic with unresolved grief and trauma; without avenues to process the abuses, many face alcoholism. Ultimately, US and Alaska government actions created these social problems by forcing assimilation onto Indigenous peoples.

Today, much of Eben's generation must carry the weight of their parents' mental health struggles. I learned much later after our trip that Eben had received news of a friend committing

---

172 William L. Iggiagruk Hensley, *Fifty Miles from Tomorrow: A Memoir of Alaska and the Real People* (New York: Picador, 2009), 70-79.

suicide while he visited Norway. Not only does Alaska have a high rate of accidental death, but it reports the highest number of suicides in the country per capita.[173] The highest suicide rates in Canada occur in Nunavut, an Inuit northern territory, and the rate in Greenland is the highest in the world. And from 2018 to 2019, the rate among Alaska Native youth nearly doubled.[174] Truly, suicide is an epidemic in the Arctic.

"Whenever I hear of a suicide that involves a young person in the North, my heart is heavy," he told me. "It feels like I failed myself because I wasn't able to be the voice they needed. We have the power to stop someone from taking their life, and I need to do better to reach out."

Any solution that could right historical wrongs would have to be culturally relevant. Iñupiaq are best fit to dictate the policies surrounding Iñupiaq, Sámi for Sámi, and so on. When they could join together in consensus, their solutions are all the more powerful and convincing. Eben wanted to become an Arctic Youth Ambassador to connect with youth around the circumpolar North. Like his *Aapa*, Grandfather, Eben wanted to build networks for Arctic people to continue fighting for their betterment.

While capitalist economies rely on values of individualism, Indigenous subsistence economies instill values of reciprocity.[175] Care and respect for even the most distant of

---

173 Statewide Suicide Prevention Council, "Alaska Suicide Facts and Statistics" (Anchorage: Alaska Department of Health and Social Services, accessed February 28, 2021).

174 Kristen Durand, "Data shows youth suicide is higher in Alaska," Alaska News Source, October 3, 2020.

175 Rauna Kuokkanen, "Indigenous Economies, Theories of Subsistence, and Women: Exploring the Social Economy Model for Indigenous Governance," *American Indian Quarterly* 35, no. 2 (Spring 2011): 215-240.

family members is of utmost importance. This is reciprocity in practice. Sacrifice, care for community.

I know from experience how the suicide of a loved one shatters your world. My first reaction to my dad's death, as a ten year old, was how selfish an act it was; to not consider how everyone else would be destroyed from losing him. But it is the opposite of that: People commit suicide when they feel there's nothing left to salvage of their life. Suicide comes from depression and disconnect with identity. It makes me angry—so angry that my fingers tremble as I type—that the government has done so little to rectify the harms caused by forced assimilation.

When Americans talk about the important policy issues in the Arctic, they usually discuss national security: the melting of the Arctic Ocean has caused military build-up in Russia. But this threat is still latent, and no one has died from it. What about the security of people who actually live in the Arctic?

The Arctic suicide epidemic is unknown to most Americans. And while America dawdles on climate change mitigation measures, we continue to contribute one-quarter of the world's carbon emissions. Like residential schools, climate change is another western creation that gnaws at traditional cultures and ways of life around the Arctic. When your identity is so closely tied with the Arctic landscape, the loss of sea ice is both deeply personal and acutely dangerous.

Arctic Indigenous peoples have adapted in the past and still retained knowledge to continue living more in tune with the land than their western counterparts. As Eben says, "I can't explain how good it feels to live as my ancestors did." Arctic Indigenous peoples have thrived in the region and will continue to thrive for the next ten thousand years.

Therefore, it is up to governments to decide where they stand. Traditionally, Alaska and Norway have developed policy solutions in rooms of white people, with maybe a couple tokenized others, because it had always been done that way; it was more convenient. Will you continue to play into that colonial pattern? Or, in the face of climate change, will you *support* young leaders like Eben in achieving self-determination?

5

WINTER

CHAPTER 14

MØRK TID

———

*Feeling secure in your worth often stems
from knowing you belong to two very special
groups: your family and your community.*

—DOROTHY S. STRICKLAND

I drove on the road between Guovdageaidnu and Tromsø many times. The fastest route took over seven hours and cut through the northern part of Finland. On either side of the Finnish border, border control was just a stoplight. If it was red, I needed to pull aside to show my passport, but the light was green on the drive back to Tromsø and I carried on at five kilometers an hour into Norway. The car's GPS showed me the Finland-Sweden border was just a few dozen kilometers away. Up north in this area, you could walk between Finland, Sweden, and Norway in one day. The landscape was all rolling hills of tundra brush; biodiverse with foxes, reindeer, and ravens; and interspersed with small villages. I continued to drive slowly, mindful that visibility was low.

Suddenly I caught a flicker of my headlights' reflection on the side of the road. The tires skidded on black ice as

I slammed on the brakes. Chill fog ensconced my view. I hoped whatever was ahead would stay there and eased my foot off the brakes.

As the car inched forward, the fog lights illuminated a few figures at a time. Twenty reindeer appeared atop the road and in the ditches on either side. Some of them had completely white fur. Others were multicolored with dark brown faces and antlers, ivory-colored shoulders, and bodies that blended in with fall tundra. Much smaller than moose, they stood only about three feet high at the shoulder. Short antlers curved from the younger ones' heads, while the stout male in the group sported a branching rack.

Honk hoooonk. Reindeer ears pricked up when I beeped the horn, but their tails swished above stationary limbs. A few lanky deer knelt snouts to lick to the asphalt. I had learned from Tuomma that they liked the taste of the anti-icing salt on the road.

Where there were reindeer, there must have been herders nearby. Siblings and cousins crossed the border to see each other weekly or monthly. Some people I knew even drove to Finland for groceries, since they did not have the 25 percent value-added tax that everything from groceries to gas did in Norway. In Kautokeino, Norway or Inari, Finland, the majority of people all spoke Northern Sámigiella. On either side of the borders, Sámi share culture, knowledge and family.

After many trips between these borders, I observed something: All this up here is Sápmi.

While few people around the world know Sámi live in northern Norway, their worldviews and culture are distinct from Norwegians. Many northern Norwegians I met at conferences would deny that difference: "My ancestors lived on this land too. Norwegians are just as Indigenous as Sámi."

But Sámi living within Norwegian borders were mandated to follow Norwegian laws and customs; it cannot be said that the opposite is true.

It's easy to become blind to injustice when you're swimming in it. With my hands on the steering wheel, I considered just how much my worldview had changed since living in Norway. When I first arrived in Tromsø, I did not understand the extent of assimilation policies in Norway, and how similar they were to the ones in Alaska. So much of that history is not written down or readily taught. I learned it by meeting new people, listening to them and trusting them. Now, it was clearer than ever before that I wouldn't find solutions to environmental justice in Norwegian governance; really, I needed to pay attention to the people in my own community who were most excluded from decision-making.

How do we unlearn the confines of the biases instilled in us? How do we create a different and more just world? I believe we will need to make changes in government policies, but many of those changes aren't politically viable—not yet. Inclusive and equitable governance will require cultural shifts, inner work, and patience for building new relationships.

As I inched the car through the herd, the reindeer trotted off the roadway. The last one lifted its snout from the road and turned its behind to me. With its tail laid on top, the deer's fluffy, white butt formed a heart shape. The image remained in my mind's eye as I carried on to Tromsø.

When I wasn't traveling north to reindeer herds in the winter, I walked to and from work through freezing rains, melty slush, feet of fresh snow, as well as slick and icy conditions on the city sidewalks. I wore a rain jacket one day and a down parka the next. Anna had wagged her finger at me when I first told her I did not own any reflective items; whenever we left the *kollektiv* together, she insisted I slap on a reflective armband on top of my coat for safety. The sun went down at 6:08 p.m. on October 1, at 2:45 p.m. on November 1, and by December, it had already disappeared beneath the horizon. Some days I shimmied down the icy hill of death leading down to my office from home, unwittingly lost my balance, and screamed out expletives as I came crashing to the street.

Having already endured prolonged winters in Anchorage, I thought I would be prepared for Tromsø's two months of darkness. Yet I was sadly mistaken. I was irritable and tired for most of *mørk tid*, the dark time. I felt the worst around Christmas, when Nora and Anna flew to Cambodia for three weeks.

Nora, Anna, her brother, and other family on her mom's side all traveled together from Tromsø to Oslo, then Dubai, and finally to Cambodia. But as Anna and her brother passed through airport security checkpoints at each airport, they were constantly pulled aside for questioning and "random" checks. Nora waited with their white family members on the clear side of security. When Anna was finally released to join them, Nora asked, "Why did they stop you?"

"I don't know," Anna said. She shook, nervous from being singled out. "The officers didn't say."

Nora began to notice the unequal ways she and Anna were received during their trip. Anna was stopped by security, and Nora was waved on ahead. The hotel required Anna's identification, but not Nora's. Waiters took Nora's order first, without even offering a glance to Anna.

Far outside Norway, Nora could see how another culture's norms affected their treatment of Anna. She finally understood what racism directed at Anna looked like. I was proud of Nora and even happier for Anna. After a four-year relationship, they could begin to unpack how racism affected their lives in Norway.

Travel can have that kind of life-changing effect. During my lonely winter days, I reminisced on the perpetually social experience I had in college. Living in North Carolina had been a continuous, four-year culture shock. I was the only person in my class from Alaska. Sometimes I talked to someone from New Jersey or Florida, and I understood their words, but we really didn't *get* each other. I felt lonely in North Carolina—and this probably sounds weird—but I liked being uncomfortable. I enjoyed being around people who were different from me because I noticed how quickly it made me grow as a person.

My very first experience at Duke was the Black Student Alliance Invitational. I was attached at the hip to a girl named Chandler, who would become my college roommate. She and I, as well as a hundred other P-froshes—pre-freshmen, just accepted into Duke—made our way up the steps of Page Auditorium. We were headed to the highlight of the Black Student Alliance Invitational: the step show.

"What is a step show?" I had whispered to Chandler in the stairwell leading to the balcony of Duke's Page Auditorium. I had no clue what that was when I read it on the program, but I was giddy with anticipation. Before we made it to the balcony and saw the stage, we could already hear dozens of high-pitched calls like boiling tea kettles, followed by booming chants: "YOUUUU KNOW!"

"It's hard to describe, but you're going to love it," she said. The boys and girls in our row were from places as diverse as California, Texas, New York, Nigeria, and Jamaica. The rows below us were filled with current students, alumni, and

members of the community. In the front rows, older gradu-
ates wore shiny, brightly colored jackets with Greek letters
down the front. The ladies in royal blue were the ones who
caught my attention.

"ZZZZZZZZZZZZ-PHI," one girl crooned. She had hair
so curly that it bounced on her shoulders with every move.
The whistle-tone sound of the letter Z sound filled the entire
auditorium. She lifted one hand up to the sky, blue sleeve
hoisted in midair. Her pinky and index fingers flexed tall
and proud, while her other fingers came together in a point.
Suddenly all the other Finer Women lifted their hands in
the same motion.

They sang back in one chorus, "Soooooooooooooooo..."

And then one after another, each of the dozens of girls
chirped in the highest octave they could reach:

"Sweet!"

"Sweet!"

"Sweet-sweet!"

When they started to step, I got lost in the sound of their
boots slamming to the stage. First one would set it off: she
exaggerated each slap on her thigh, stomp of her foot, clap
above her head with sultry movements. Each sorority girl
joined in, making tight, strong movements, their limbs at
forty-five and ninety degree angles.

I had seen movies about fraternities where primarily
white college students threw crazy parties. And while historically Black Greek-letter organizations (BGLOs) were a
critical part of Duke's Black social life—for better or for worse,
considering that Black women are just as affected by sexual
assault as white sorority girls—partying wasn't what they
were all about. From hosting community-building events on
campus to leading service activities, it seemed that being in

a Black sorority was first and foremost about being a leader in the Black community.

From the moment I stepped onto campus, I knew I wanted to be part of that. Being Black was always a crucial part of my identity, but people hadn't seen me as I saw myself back back home. A college professor explained it to me once: He said the color of one's skin is the first thing we see. Without trying, our brains immediately decide how to approach a person based on our implicit biases about their race. People approach a Black man differently than a white man and, in my case, people don't know how to approach me. I had to define my identity for myself to show them who I was.

At Duke, I did not find that people were any less racist than in Alaska. In my four short years, a tenured professor published an op-ed stating that Black people "just feel sorry for themselves," unlike Asians who choose "simple American" names for their children.[176] Someone scribbled "nigger" on the flyer advertising a Patrisse Cullors talk (one of the founders of Black Lives Matter) hosted by The Mary Lou Williams Center for Black Culture, so the flyer read "The Mary Lou Williams Center for Nigger Culture."[177] Then the vice president of the university allegedly hit a Black parking guard with his car and called her the N-word too.[178] When I was a senior, things came full circle. The man in charge of student affairs ended up getting a Black woman fired for

---

176 Karthick Ramakrishnan, "'Strange' vs. 'simple old '"American' names," The Chicago Tribune, May 28, 2015.

177 Mumbi N. Kanyogo, "Anonymous Anti-Blackness and Institutional Racism," in Duke Disorientation Guide 2018, September 9, 2018.

178 Susan Svrluga, "Duke official apologizes for lack of 'civility' in parking dispute as sit-in over racial slur continues," The Washington Post, April 4, 2016.

playing a song with the N-word on the radio in the coffee shop at the Bryan Center.[179]

The difference was having a like-minded community with whom to process those scandals. Among other Black students, I could discuss the racism I experienced at home and at Duke without being questioned. When I complained that my professors were underestimating me, the answer was, "Girl, I know." When I talked about the racist assumptions that underlie white culture, it was, "Well, yeah." *Duh.*

Three years after that first step show, I found myself waiting behind the curtain at Page Auditorium, a member of Zeta Phi Beta Sorority, Inc. Hundreds of seventeen- and eighteen-year-olds perched in the balcony, enraptured. When all the lights went out, my chapter and I ran out and filed into a line at center stage. We donned blue work shirts, jeans, jackets, and hats like the gardener in *Get Out*, since the movie was the theme for our performance. When the lights came on again, the entire audience erupted in cheers and shouts of adoration.

I suppressed a smile with a grit face: both corners of my mouth downturned toward my chin, a vein popped out the right side of my neck and my eyes bored deep into the crowd. When the audio clip played, we all fanned out from the line taking heavy, intentional steps with choreographed sounds along the way. In unison, our right hands slapped our left hands, then right thighs; we bent down and clapped under our knees, then sprung back up and stomped on the ground. It all produced a powerful ensemble. *Get Out* uses metaphor to describe the consumption of Black culture and

---

179 Abbie Bennett, "Campus coffee shop was playing rap. Duke VP's complaint got employees fired, IndyWeek reports," The News & Observer, May 9, 2018.

assimilation of Black people in America and, at a primarily white institution, the performance was even more meaningful.

"Okaaay, Michaela!" my brother from Phi Beta Sigma Fraternity Inc. called out from the audience.

I gained confidence in my perspectives around other Black people. My hesitancy to showcase my voice, myself, was built into the experiences I had at school in Alaska. My classmates, every single one of my teachers in middle and elementary school, and most of them in high school were white. For most of my upbringing, my dad wasn't able to teach me how to be Black and proud. I had to be intentional about building up my identity.

When I came to Norway, I put myself right back into an all-white environment. And as unprepared as I was for *mørk tid*, I was even less prepared for the isolating effects of racism. Many winter Saturdays were spent horizontal in bed, glazed-over eyes binge-watching Netflix. I spent more time indoors and alone, and the isolation only deepened my seasonal affective disorder (SAD). SAD has a way of sneaking up on you: Something makes you sad, you think you're constantly sad about that one thing, and don't realize how the sadness has leaked into every moment of your days. It's not until the sun begins to rise that suddenly things seem bearable again, and you wonder what you were so tired and angry for.

On the surface, I blamed Norway for all the reasons I felt sad and alone. I found it difficult to enjoy Norwegian food because it paled in comparison to the diversity and availability of American food; but really because eating constantly reminded me of my favorite foods from home. I reviled at the difficulty in making friends because a working life was far less social than college, regardless of where I lived. I hated that I could not wear my hair down or dress how I wanted without attracting comments or stares. Beneath the surface, the things I disliked were linked to a larger struggle.

Living in Norway confounded me, like a pressure cooker for my identity. I missed that feeling I had gained and lost: confidence. I was constantly considering how privileged I was to be here, often feeling like a foreigner who could never belong, and all those thoughts were so numerous that they could fill an entire book.

Of course, Anna had toed this line her whole life. Later in 2019, after the sun came back and I paid my ticket, she began to consider what life would be like had she grown up outside Norway. We visited a grocery store together, just the two of us. After walking up and down every aisle, checking out, and leaving the store, I made the offhand comment: "Do you realize we were the only non-white people in the whole store?"

She was quiet for a moment, lips parted, before she replied, "*Herregud.* I didn't even notice."

Anna had rarely had the opportunity to make friends who were accustomed to more diversity. So, when strangers at work told her to go back to where she came from or coworkers doubted her intelligence, no one around had the vocabulary to tell her those things were racist.

I felt similarly when I was younger. There was a lot of diversity in Anchorage, but still the vast majority of people were white. The many different ethnicities of people of color in Anchorage made up very small communities dispersed across one of the biggest municipalities in the country. I did not have the confidence or vocabulary to identify every act of racism against me, either, because all my experiences taught me *this is just how people like me are treated.*

"Imagine how things would be different if people told you, sooner, you didn't deserve to be treated that way," I told Anna.

"I still think about that conversation," she told me recently.

I encouraged Anna to visit me in America, so she would have the opportunity to be around more dark-skinned people one day. Those experiences are what gave me the vocabulary to talk about racism and what treatment I will not tolerate. I hope Anna gained that, at least a little, from our relationship.

Like the sun for SAD, meaningful relationships helped me imagine myself and my history in new ways—that inner work is always ongoing. At the same time, my new friends learned a lot from me. But it had taken years to build that confidence. I believe we should intentionally love dark-skinned and Indigenous people as individuals, as well as collectives. Creating relationships with new people is the most enriching part of travel but, if we want to grow beyond our own worldviews, it's also something we need to be doing at home.

CHAPTER 15

JUST TRANSITION

The cost of liberty is less than the price of repression.

—W. E. B. DU BOIS

When the sun came back to the Arctic in 2019, my desperate feelings of hopelessness faded into the horizon like the rain clouds of November and December. The many compounding feet of fluffy snowflakes accumulated on roads, on cars, on rooftops, clinging to my hair on walks to the grocery store and freezing onto tree branches; deep snow amplified the sun's light and the shimmering highlights of the ocean. Suddenly the streets were more crowded with northerners emerging from their dens, more chipper with sounds of many birds returning to town. I saw people carrying skis around, studs crunching ice under boots, young couples holding hands under the grand holiday lights strung up along the Walking Street. The winter wonderland of sun and snow set a trance upon Tromsø.

I took advantage of the beautiful time with Chilon and Michelle, an Inuk researcher from Canada who interned at the Indigenous Peoples' Secretariat. Our friendships entailed cultural differences but, in my opinion, our motley crew shared more similarities than we even imagined at the time.

I liked Michelle immediately. She came from a small town called Happy Valley–Goose Bay and carried that charm everywhere we went; she was as cheery as you'd imagine someone from Happy Valley might be and as goofy as a goose. Both of us inevitably insisted on holding the door open when we walked through doorways together. "Go ahead," Michelle said, cheeks flexing as she smiled. "No, you first," I would offer. "Ladies first!" Michelle responded. We would carry on with this polite fight until someone who wasn't North American pushed through the open door.

When I first introduced Chilon and Michelle, we drove north along the coast of Tromsdalen until Tromsøya's city lights faded to the horizon. Past 8 p.m., and the sun had already set two hours before. Chilon's hands rested on the steering wheel, and he remarked that the last time he drove out here was during the day.

"I wanted to see the little towns... Tønsvik, Oldervik, Breivik." He glanced at Michelle and me, crowded into the passenger and middle seat in the truck's front seat. "You know *vik* means bay in Norwegian." I imagined Chilon in the scarf, beanie, and peacoat he often wore, towering over the locals in those coastal towns. The further on the periphery of Norway, the more strictly Norwegian social rules would be enforced. He guffawed. "You should have seen their faces when they heard me speaking Norwegian. No one could look away from my beautiful face."

Chilon, Michelle, and I ventured out here to see the aurora borealis. Michelle rolled down the window and searched the sky. "Wait," she gasped. "Let's park!"

Chilon rolled into an empty lot stacked with shipping containers turned into temporary units where construction workers slept during extended projects. I lifted my hood and zipped the parka, which made me look like a jumbo-sized marshmallow, Chilon wrapped his scarf around his face, while Michelle donned a windbreaker and not much else. Prepped for the outdoors, we climbed down from the truck and walked beyond it, away from the light source in the parking lot.

The aurora borealis was rarely visible in Anchorage because of the city's light pollution. Only when the sky is dark can you see the dreamy light inspired by collisions between the sun's streams of electrically charged particles, oxygen, and nitrogen in Earth's atmosphere.[180] The aurora only occurs at the poles because the planet's magnetic field pushes the solar particles there. High up north and a bit outside the city, Troms was one of the most accessible places worldwide to experience such a show.

Directly above us, green flaming tendrils rippled and whirled across the star-speckled sky. Wind whipped around our heads while all three of us stood open-mouthed, gaping at the magnificent view. The northern lights moved like a dance ribbon, rippling back and forth in waves. Then parts of the ribbon would branch off, creating a chorus of lights the brightest electric green you can imagine. The solar flares must have included hydrogen or helium, because purple streams of light began to appear in the minutes we stood there.

"I never seen them this clear and crazy," Michelle remarked, hands casually tucked in her windbreaker's pockets.

---

180 *National Geographic Resource Library*, s.v. "Aurora," last updated May 14, 2011.

The lights continued dancing, expanding and shooting across the ceiling. After fifteen minutes in the freezing weather, Chilon and I began to shiver. Michelle was barely phased; the Labrador and Newfoundland province she came from was further south than Troms, but thirty degrees Fahrenheit colder in average winter months.[181]

With two Inuit parents, Michelle grew up on the land. On Canada's Thanksgiving weekend, she used to go hunting with her family. All the cousin children would take turns practicing with bows, and every morning she and her cousin were tasked to hunt for partridges. Partridges are the same bird as ptarmigans, the Alaska state bird, and they're known for being so daft that you could walk up to one and catch it with your bare hands. But instead of a partridge, she and her cousin always came back with a bucket of blueberries or raspberries.

"I'm tough as nails now, but I was kind of squeamish as a kid," Michelle laughed. "My mom used to tease, 'She's more of a gatherer than a hunter.'"

When Michelle finally started to feel cold and Chilon couldn't handle the wind anymore, we made our way back to the car. In the car ride to town, Chilon asked Michelle why she came to Norway. At the Indigenous Peoples' Secretariat, she was most interested in the use of Indigenous knowledge in the Arctic Council's research.

"Studying biology at university for the past four years, I noticed a lot of things that I learned from growing up on the land, and traditional knowledge in general, were missing from the curriculum," Michelle said, warming her hands in front of the car's vent.

---

181 "Happy Valley-Goose Bay, NL, Canada Weather averages," Google, accessed April 2, 2021.

Back home, Michelle led a team in documenting photos and stories about birds in Nunatsiavut, the very first Inuit land claims area established in Canada. After learning traditional names and stories about birds from Nunatsiavummiut, the Inuit who live in that region, her research team ultimately published a book called *A Nunatsiavut Field Guide to the Birds of Labrador*.[182] Nunatsiavummiut achieve a level of self-determination under the Nunatsiavut government; it is still a part of Newfoundland and Labrador government, but has the ability to make laws about health, education, justices, community governance, culture, and language in the region.[183]

Michelle knew firsthand that such arrangements had their limits. On a family vacation in Alberta, Michelle's family had visited the "Badlands," where the Canadian government did not allow humans to touch the ancient rock formations. But Michelle still loves to scream, "I'm from Labrador!" from the rooftops, and her Inuit culture was just as important to her dad. Traditionally, Inuit built landmarks called *inukshuk* as they traveled across the land. Her dad gathered loose rocks and stacked them atop one another, forming two legs at the base, a torso and a head to communicate with other Inuit travelers. When environmental managers caught him, they nearly called in RCMP, the Royal Canadian Mounted Police, to arrest him.

It is important to note that the RCMP was originally founded to enforce the transfer of Indigenous territories to

---

182 Michelle Saunders, "A Nunatsiavut Field Guide to the Birds of Labrador," Tradition and Transition, September 2018.

183 "Nunatsiavut," Tradition and Transition, accessed March 28, 2021.

the federal government by relocating people, forcing them to stay on reservations during famines, and warring with people who did not submit. In Canada today, the RCMP kills Indigenous people at ten times the rate of white people.[184]

Working at the Arctic Council, Michelle and I were able to meet Sámi, Dene (Athabaskan), Unangax (Aleut), Gwich'in, and Inuit from Greenland and to Russia who shared similar experiences. They were fighting to practice their culture in their homelands, to include their multigenerational knowledge in Arctic biodiversity management and climate change action, and to have some control over the lands they always stewarded. And while people in the Arctic share these experiences, they are linked to global systems of colonialism and exploitative capitalism.

"What about you, Chilon?" she asked. "What brought you here?"

"I'm from the Congo," he answered, eyes on the road. With one hand, he gestured toward the homes and peaceful scene outside the truck. "It's one of the poorest and richest countries in the world. I wish my country would be like others, but I don't think I will see it in my lifetime. Powers in the West will leave us in chaos to keep control over the minerals especially."

From outside the Congo, Chilon only saw media that depicted Africans as dumb, poor, or bloodthirsty. In this Arctic setting, his name, manner of speaking, and physical presence were striking. It seemed that Norwegians would do anything to make him fade into the background. At the clubs, drunk Norwegian boys called him names, trying to

---

184 Amnesty International Canada, "Black and Indigenous Solidarity Against Systemic Racism," *Human Rights Now* (blog), July 20, 2020.

test him or pick a fight. Eventually Chilon learned not to tolerate that kind of treatment.

The refugee crisis and postcolonial warfare that brought Chilon to Norway can be traced back to the eve of Congolese independence in 1960.[185] When he began to research the history of his country, he found plenty of evidence that colonizing nations had vested interests in opposing his people's self-governance and self-determination. Chilon continued, "My proudest achievement is knowing myself and my roots as a Black man."

When Chilon was barely a figment of his parents' imagination, a young leader named Patrice Lumumba gained a large following in the Congo. He advocated for pan-African independence among the many Black peoples living under Belgium's violent, capitalist rule. For more than two hundred years, Belgians had extracted raw minerals and free, forced labor from the previous stewards of that land. During the Cold War, the United States sought strategic control over raw minerals across the world, and Belgium was convinced that the United States was planning to usurp their colonial control.[186] When Patrice Lumumba came to power and declared intentions to liberate Congo from all colonizers, the US and Belgium both developed plans to assassinate a leader whom Chilon's parents supported.[187]

---

185 Georges Nzongola-Ntalaja, *The Congo from Leopold to Kabila: A People's History* (United Kingdom: Bloomsbury Academic, 2002), 3.

186 The Woodrow Wilson International Center for Scholars' Cold War International History Project and Africa Program, *The Congo Crisis, 1960-1961: A Critical Oral History Conference* (Washington, DC: Woodrow Wilson International Center for Scholars, 2004), 23.

187 *Encyclopaedia Britannica Online*, Academic ed., s.v. "How did Patrice Lumumba die?," accessed March 28, 2021.

In one of the most important assassinations of the twentieth century, a competing Congolese political party allied with the United States and Belgium killed Lumumba just seven months after independence.[188] The event rocked the new nation, and its government has never since gained stability. Today, American companies still profit from resources extracted by armed factions in the Congo—companies only need to report which products incorporate minerals that are *not* "DRC conflict free."[189]

"We are living in a world where people are like wolves," Chilon said, eyes fiery. With only the passing streetlights periodically illuminating the car, I could still see how deeply personal this history was to Chilon. Deep lines formed canyons between his brows as he finished: "The rich get richer, and the poor get poorer."

Those inequities—disproportionate control over land, resources and power—are the root of environmental injustice. Because many Indigenous and Black peoples have been displaced and our lands dispossessed, we don't have economic or political control over our environments. This is also why we see unfair wealth in the hands of white, western people.

One of the biggest misconceptions in our world is that current inequalities are just destiny; that individualism and greed are human nature. But these conditions were created in rooms full of white men with western world views. If more Black and Indigenous people had access to decision-making power and knowledge about our peoples' histories, I hope we could build a different world.

---

188 Georges Nzongola-Ntalaja, "Patrice Lumumba: the most important assassination of the 20th century," *The Guardian*, January 17, 2011.

189 Nicholas Cook, *Conflict Minerals in Central Africa: US and International Responses* (Washington, DC: Congressional Research Service, 2012).

I fully believe that we are capable of transitioning to new types of economies and governance that treat Black and Indigenous peoples equitably. As humans move into the future, we need to:

- Advance community control over resources, especially by redistributing extreme wealth.
- Re-localize production and consumption.
- Move from militarized police states to governments of deep democracy, where realities on the margins of society are as important to decision-making as majority rule.
- Retain, restore, and develop cultures and traditions, particularly of Black and Indigenous peoples.
- Restore ecological balance by replacing the colonial, consumerist mindsets with reciprocity and sacredness.[190]

Of course, we aren't taught how to do this in schools. We need to begin by learning the histories of the places we live and grew up in. Through our relationships with other Black and Indigenous peoples, we can build even more knowledge about the systems of oppression that connect us.[191]

We know the colonial foundation for our current state was laid centuries ago. It may be centuries more before white supremacy disappears. So, as individuals, we can't always bear the weight of the world on our shoulders. We all need

---

190 Climate Justice Alliance, "Just Transition: A Framework for Change," accessed March 28, 2021.

191 Native Peoples Action, "An Indigenous Vision for Our Collective Future: Becoming Earth's Stewards Again," Nonprofit Quarterly (Fall 2020).

rest to recharge. Personally, I have to remind myself that I am worthy of laughter, relaxation, and joy.

Later in March, Chilon borrowed a truck from his friend to drive all three of us out to the pier in a nearby village where no one would be around. Bathing suits under our clothes, towels and blankets piled up in the backseat, Chilon parked the truck at the dock. He turned and locked eyes with us.

"Are you sure you want to do this, crazy girls?"

"What, you think this is my first time swimming in the Arctic Ocean?" I retorted. I'd run into the water on the North Slope of Alaska before I'd even left for Duke and again along the rocky shore where our study abroad group had stayed in Nuuk, Greenland. I wasn't going to leave Tromsø without dipping in the cold sea.

"Okay, everyone, take your clothes off. It's now or never," Michelle said.

I squealed and giggled, and Chilon huffed in fake exasperation. We stored our pants and shirts in the truck trailer, each grabbed a towel and shoved our bare feet in boots, then skittered across the wooden boards in the cover of night. A storefront, closed for the day, was the only building around; a couple empty rescue boats floated off the opposite side of the dock. The three of us lined up along the opposite edge, knees knocking against one another, foggy exhales escaping our lips.

"It's not too late to turn back—" Chilon started, teeth chattering.

But I cannonballed before he finished, sending a splash soaring above the clear, endlessly dark depths. An electric shock jolted through my toes to my shoulders as the sea engulfed me in salt water. I pumped my arms and kicked my legs hard, churning water and floating. Michelle and Chilon cheered from the dock.

The temperature in these waters was about 4.6 degrees Celsius (40.3 degrees Fahrenheit).[192] For swimming, this temperature can be extremely cold and dangerous. But it's a well-known Scandinavian tradition and an energy-booster to dip into the freezing water for a few moments. Some people even wear hats to stop from losing too much heat.

"I'm coming!" Michelle made a running start and flung herself in the water.

"I guess it is good to be open-minded," Chilon yelled. Finally, he doubled back, looked away, and hopped in upright like a two-meter-tall needle.

Chilon was a proponent that the best type of people is those who know themselves well enough to be open-minded about different characters from various religions, races, and genders. To see and acknowledge difference, not judge, and carry on living life.

I swam the breaststroke around the little section before the cold started to make me short of breath, then located the ladder hanging off the dock and pulled myself back on shore. One after another, we wrapped towels around ourselves and jogged back to the car, a breeze sweeping past our freezing, red ears. Chilon turned the key in the ignition and ratcheted the heat up to high. We wrapped more blankets around our bodies while we dried, covered up in sweat pants and heavy shirts, and headed back to town.

---

192 "February weather forecast and climate: Tromsø, Norway," Weather Atlas, accessed February 17, 2021._

EPILOGUE

So when I made up my mind to do my best to shine
some light on the Arctic and on the story of a people
most Americans barely know exist, I didn't hesitate.
—WILLIAM L. IĠĠIAĠRUK HENSLEY

Although I sought the solutions for justice in equitable countries like Iceland and Norway, I did not find them there. The
friends I made had faced systemic racism, and their experiences felt familiar to my own. From Norway to Alaska to the
Congo, white decision-makers excluded Indigenous peoples
from decision-making processes about their own homelands.
They used assimilation projects to separate us from the very
core of our identities. And today, Black and Indigenous peoples are still not adequately represented in decision-making bodies or provided rightful control over their land and
resources. In the Arctic, the manifestation of environmental
injustice are policies that destroy the relationships people have
with the land, their communities, and themselves.

To me, it seems the driving force behind the injustice is white supremacy. Notions of property ownership,

growth-based capitalism and manifest destiny are the very root of our most essential challenges, including climate change. We need to be explicit and honest about confronting ongoing inequity, assimilation, and colonialism in the Arctic, and around the world, because decision-makers still have not made space for worldviews that come from outside historically white institutions.

On January 6, 2021, I was back in Alaska. Five months before, I began working at a policy think tank called the Polar Institute—dubbed the "Arctic Public Square" by Senators and international diplomats. I was supposed to move to Washington, DC for the job, but the COVID-19 pandemic broke out in 2020, just months after I returned to Alaska from Norway. I had just signed into my virtual workspace from an at-home desk in my family's living room while the news played on the TV. For the moment, I was glad I did not have to be in the nation's capital.

"We are getting reports that protesters have entered the Capitol," the news reporters declared.

"Family, come look at this," I yelled.

My mom's boyfriend got up from the dining room table and my mom came from her desk. We all gaped at the Confederate flags entering the building, the wall-climber dressed in all black. Terrorists chanted about killing the vice president, sat in senators' chairs, and fought the small handful of police officers tasked with holding them back.

"This thing looks staged," Mom's boyfriend said.

"I mean, yeah…," I responded.

It was clearly an intended coup, if poorly executed. Trump tweeted his followers to stop Congress from certifying Joe Biden as the presidential election winner, and a broad base of primarily white people with white-collar jobs organized at the Capitol.[193] There were videos of police officers who opened the gates for rioters, and thirty-five US Capitol officers were investigated for supporting their cause.[194] The riot got so out of hand because the President did not call in the National Guard, as he was so quick to do in other cities that summer. When the DC mayor requested the Guard, the Pentagon refused to issue the DC National Guard to the scene because of the "optics."[195] The news called the whole thing a "peaceful protest" for much of the morning, but it looked eerily like a lynch mob that those in the Trump administration supported.

It was also a stark example of white privilege at force: The terrorists had the support of the president. There's only been one Black president. Yet President Obama could achieve little to broach inequality in America, since white rage and backlash curtailed him at every step. Racism inspired, for example, one of the federal government's biggest shutdowns in history over the Affordable Care Act.[196]

I showed my family the photo of the Capitol steps the day of the Black Lives Matter protest mere months earlier. There were rows upon rows of armed officers lining the Capitol steps. Watching the footage on TV, Black people knew how we would have been treated had we been in those rioters' shoes. There would have been bodies.

---

193 Robert A. Pape and Keven Ruby. "The Capitol Rioters Aren't Like Other Extremists," The Atlantic, February 2, 2021.

194 Richard Cowen, "US Capitol Police investigating role of 35 officers during January 6 riot," Reuters, February 19, 2021.

195 Paul Sonne, Peter Hermann and Missy Ryan, "Pentagon placed limits on DC Guard ahead of pro-Trump protests due to narrow mission," The Washington Post, January 7, 2021.

196 Paul Waldman, "Yes, Opposition to Obamacare is Tied Up with Race," Plum Line (blog), The Washington Post, May 23, 2014.

White supremacy does present a clear threat to demo-graphically changing societies. A study by Syracuse University and Military Times found that about 48 percent of more than 1,000 surveyed listed white nationalists as a significant national security threat. This was nearly the same amount who considered al-Qaida to be a significant national security threat.[197]

In the July 22 terrorist attack on Oslo, a white nationalist terrorist murdered nearly eighty people during attacks against the government office complex in Oslo and Labour Party youth camp on Utøya. According to the memorial center I visited, the terrorist was incensed by the government's "secret 'multicultural project,' believing that ethnic Norwegians had been subjected to abuse in the form of ethnic 'deconstruction' since the Norwegian Labour Party opened up the possibility of mass immigration during the 1960s."[198]

Yet the event did not cause the government to take broad action against racism. Similar to much of the media after the January 6 insurrection, news articles and op-eds concentrated on strengthening policing and public security.[199] The terrorists in both countries believed they were the nations' rightful people. Yet Norway and America both avoided the necessary discussion on ethnicity and whiteness.

When I point out the racism in Norway, Alaska, and the rest of the United States, it's not just for fun. Everyday white supremacy is presenting an immediate threat to security, health, and opportunity for millions around the world. Colonialism, its sister, continues to lay the grounds for global

197 Leo Shane III, "Troops: White nationalism a national security threat equal to ISIS, al-Qaida," *Military Times*, September 3, 2020.

198 22. juli-senteret, "The 22nd of July 2011," accessed February 17, 2021.

199 Åshild Kolås, "How critical is the event? Multicultural Norway after 22 July 2011," *Taylor & Francis Online* 23, no. 5 (January 2017): 518-532.

inequity and environmental degradation. It is time, has always been the time, that white people begin to confront their own notions of supremacy. It will take a more diverse set of world views and decision-makers to fashion a more just world.

That's why, when my Hart Leadership Fellowship ended in May 2019, I moved back to Tromsø as an Indigenous Peoples' Secretariat (IPS) Associate at the Arctic Council Secretariat after a two-month summer back in Anchorage, Alaska. I primarily worked on projects like the 6th Arctic Leaders' Summit—acting as the point of contact between IPS, the six Indigenous peoples' organizations and invited participants—and Ságastallamin, a large-scale exhibition about revitalization initiatives for Indigenous languages around the Arctic.[200] My term ended in December 2019, just before COVID broke out in 2020.

In my travels around the Arctic, I was most enraptured by the plethora of talent, brains, and leadership among Indigenous and Black youth. The fact that high-level representation in Arctic environmental decision-making does not look like them is a testament to ongoing racism and discrimination in the North. Many of the answers we are looking for already exist, but unequal representation in decision-making and an addiction to growth-based capitalism stops decision-makers from taking action.

My friends Chilon, Anna, Nora, and Susie showed me that building strong relationships between Black peoples, Indigenous peoples and beyond is the way to break out of the colonial norms we've internalized. Although it may take generations for white peoples to learn that we matter, we already know it in our hearts. When we rely on each other, we can make a much greater impact than we would alone.

---

200 "Ságastallamin – Telling the story of Arctic Indigenous languages," UiT The Arctic University of Norway University Library, accessed April 2, 2021.

People like Michelle, Ole-Ante, Eben, and Ture-Bie-htar made me feel less alone in fighting climate change. In particular, Black and Indigenous peoples are at the helm of reimagining what our world could look like. Knowing your food, environment, and community is independence. It allows you to thrive in the face of global change without the government's support. Moving from the land to urban environments weathers our resilience.[201] One of my goals in life is to produce whatever food I can and begin to rely primarily on local hunters, fishers and gatherers—partic-ularly Black and Indigenous small businesses—rather than grocery stores.

Moreover, I think Eben has the right idea: Cross-border collaboration among Arctic youth is an important way to create a better future. In my new position at the Wilson Cen-ter's Polar Institute, one of the initiatives I'm most proud to have started is an Arctic Youth Symposium. In May 2021, it centered young Arctic practitioners, traditional knowledge holders, and scholars in one of the world's top-ten think tanks.[202] I don't think the solutions to climate change and racism will come with a quick or technical fix. It will take a culture shift, particularly among the white collar and deci-sion-making classes to relinquish control over lands. The very first step in a culture shift, before deep relationships or policy change, is exposure to new information.

In one of my final trips before returning to Alaska, I attended a large Arctic conference in St. Petersburg, Russia.

---

201 Wilfred Greaves, "Cities and Human Security in a Warming Arctic," in *Climate Change and Arctic Security*, eds. Lassi Heininen and Heather Exner-Pirot (New York: Palgrave Pivot, 2020), 61-89.

202 Ryan McKenna, "The Wilson Center Once Again Named A Top 10 Think Tank Worldwide," Wilson Center press release, January 28, 2021.

Since the Russian Federation would assume leadership at the Arctic Council in 2021, I'd learned some basic Russian words at my job the last few months. On the spring Saturday morning I wasn't rushing from session to session, I scheduled a tattoo appointment. The grungy tattoo artist with spiky blond hair and his black-haired girlfriend unlocked his basement tattoo shop in a graffitied apartment block.

Before arriving at the shop, I'd sent the artist my ideas for the tattoo: the northern part of the globe decorated around the edges with crowberries, a little watery black berry that grew in the mountains in every Arctic country. As of 2019 I had traveled to them all: Iceland, Norway, Denmark via Greenland, Sweden, Finland, Canada, the USA, and the Russian Federation. I wanted to celebrate having achieved more in my short life than I ever would have imagined growing up. People always tried to define me based on how I looked physically, and here was the physical manifestation of a region that shaped me more than their misunderstanding ever could.

After three hours of stabbing ink into my thigh, my leg started to jump at the needle without my mind's permission. I glanced down at the outline of the berry; blood oozed, and I felt the ghost tremor of the needle. Though we'd spoken all of ten words since I arrived at the tattoo shop, I struck up a conversation to distract from the pain. I had learned a trick in Norway: I spoke English into an audio app, showed the translated Russian on my phone screen, then switched the language so he could communicate with me. I told him I was in town for a conference, and that I'd be back in another month for a summit in Arkhangelsk, архангельск.

"архангельск!" he exclaimed. His eyebrows shot up, and he pulled the tattoo gun away from my thigh.

The tattoo artist was shocked I knew of his hometown. Like me, he'd come from the North. The Arctic town was a few hundred years old and built almost entirely out of wood. Even the sidewalk near the dormitory I stayed in was made of wood, squelching and crumbling underfoot.

He typed some words into his phone and handed the translation to me: "Most people in Russia don't even know about Arkhangelsk."

I laughed out loud. I'd heard so many crazy assumptions about Alaska from Americans: Do we ride moose to school? Live in igloos? Isn't Alaska an island in the Pacific Ocean? Most people in America couldn't guess what Alaska is really like, nor do people in Oslo understand life for Sámi in Arctic Norway.

But for people who have always lived in the region, continuing their ancestors' traditions is a source of pride and identity. By continuing to hunt, fish, herd, and gather in traditional ways, Indigenous peoples provide a great service to the Arctic environment and the world at large. But many southerners imagine the Arctic to be a cold, barren wasteland.

If readers take anything away from this book, I hope it is a deeper adoration for the Arctic, the people who live there, and their many ethnicities and cultures. If you are from the North, I hope you felt seen. The outside world, down to our very own governments, turns a blind eye to northerners' existence all too often.

Zzzzzzzzzzzzzzzzzzzz. The tattoo artist started up again, ink dripping from the end of the needle. I took a deep breath. For the first hour of the tattoo, my mom had talked to me on the phone. But the time difference was ten hours from Anchorage, even further than Norway, and she fell asleep early on. Like most types of pain, it was worse when I tried to fight it alone.

GLOSSARY

ANTHROPOCENE
The current geological age, in which human activity is the dominant influence on climate and the environment.

ÁRBEDIEHTU
Sámi traditional knowledge.

ARCTIC COUNCIL
The Arctic Council is the leading intergovernmental forum promoting cooperation, coordination and interaction among the Arctic States, Arctic Indigenous peoples, and other Arctic inhabitants on common Arctic issues. The Permanent Participant organizations representing Arctic Indigenous peoples; organizations and non-Arctic states called Observers; and Member states of the Arctic Council primarily work on Arctic issues of sustainable development and environmental protection in the Council's Working Groups. The Arctic Council's mandate, as articulated in the Ottawa Declaration of 1996, explicitly excludes military security.[203]

---

203 "About the Arctic Council," Arctic Council, accessed March 28, 2021.

BLACKNESS

Enterprise community says: Black people are not a monolith and Black communities are not monolithic. Blackness is expansive enough to accommodate the experiences of women, LGBTQIA, Latinx, the differently abled, business owners, parents, those with varying degrees of education, immigrants, the many Black ethnicities and much more. White supremacy and racism rely on the perception and perpetuation of Black people as a single and narrowly defined group; centering Blackness allows for honoring the full humanity of Black people and the complexity of identities.[204]

DUOTTAR

Tundra in the North Sámi language.

FORNORSK

Most literally, "Norwegianization." The Norwegian government employed a set of policies from the 1920s up until the 1990s intended to assimilate Sámi people.[205]

KOLLEKTIV

A shared household where residents play a full part, from cleaning to social events. A popular living option among students and young people in Norwegian cities, also increasingly efficient and socially expedient for professionals.[206]

---

204 Chandra Christmas-Rouse, Brandon C. Jones and Meghan Venable-Thomas, *Building to Heal: A Framework for Holistic Community Development* (Enterprise Community: December 2020), 7.

205 Henry Minde, "The Norwegianization of the Sami — why, how and what consequences?," in *Sámi skuvlahistorjá 1*, eds. Svein Lund, Elfrid Boine and Siri Broch Johansen (Kárášjohka/Karasjok: Davvi Girji, 2005).

206 David Nikel, "Renting a House in Norway," *Norway Weekly* (blog), Life in Norway, March 3, 2017.

INDIGENEITY

According to the UN Permanent Forum on Indigenous Issues, Indigeneity constitutes:

- Self-identification as Indigenous at the individual level and acceptance by the community as their member
- Historical continuity with pre-colonial and/or pre-settler societies
- Strong link to territories and surrounding natural resources
- Distinct social, economic or political systems
- Distinct language, culture and beliefs
- Form non-dominant groups of society
- Resolve to maintain and reproduce their ancestral environments and systems as distinctive peoples and communities[207]

LAND USE CHANGE

The transformation of land from one land use type to another (such as forests, cropland, grazing land, industrial development, and permanent residences) primarily via human and economic activities.[208] Soil rich with trees and other organisms stores carbon underground, and land use change resulting in the removal of natural habitat causes atmospheric carbon emissions that contribute to climate change.[209] Land use change is a leading threat to biodiversity.[210]

---

207 United Nations Permanent Forum on Indigenous Issues, *Who are indigenous peoples?*, factsheet, accessed March 12, 2021.

208 ScienceDirect "Land Use Change," accessed March 11, 2021.

209 UNFCCC Secretariat, "Land Use, Land-Use Change and Forestry," United Nations Climate Change, accessed March 11, 2021.

210 Martin Jung, Pedram Rowhani, and Jörn P. W. Scharlemann, "Impacts of past abrupt land change on local biodiversity globally," *Nature Communications* 10, no. 5474 (2019).

LAVVU
A traditional Sámi tent.

LYSGÅRDEN
The roofed courtyard inside the newer addition to the Fram Centre (Framsenteret) in Tromsø, Norway: Fram II.

MØRKHUDET
Dark-skinned, an adjective in Norwegian.

RACISM
The individual and systemic subordination and dehumanization of non-white people, supported by cultural norms and values, the actions of individuals, and society's institutional structures and practices.[211] Racism is founded upon and perpetuated by the underpaid labor and undervalued land of non-white people, and of Black and Indigenous peoples in particular. Racism is not just an individual's biases, but a quantifiable reality embedded in systems.

SÁMIGIELLA
The North Sámi language.

SELF-DETERMINATION
The right of a people to freely determine their political status and freely pursue their economic, social and cultural development. All peoples have the right to self-determination.[212]

---

211 Charmaine L. Wijeyesinghe, Pat Griffin, and Barbara Love, "Racism-Curriculum Design," in *Teaching for Diversity and Social Justice*, eds. Maurianne Adams, Lee Anne Bell, and Pat Griffin (New York: Routledge, 1997), 88-99.

212 "2200A (XXI). International Covenant on Economic, Social and Cultural Rights," Office of the High Commissioner on Human Rights, United Nations, entered into force January 3, 1976.

SIIDA

Kinship-based communities of Sámi reindeer herders; the customary units of managing reindeer herds.[213]

UTLENDING

Foreigners, a noun in Norwegian.

WHITENESS

Whiteness is a boundary with varying levels of flexibility that separates "those who are entitled to have certain privileges from those whose exploitation and vulnerability to violence is justified by their not being white."[214] The boundary sometimes relies on skin color, other times in accordance with the norms and values associated with "white" ethnicities.

WHITE SUPREMACY

The belief that white people are superior to other races and should dominate society. White supremacy is also the reality that white people currently occupy disproportionate power, privilege and wealth. For example, in the United States white people make up 92.6 percent of Fortune 500 CEOs, over 80 percent of nonprofit directors, and 88 percent of Senior Executive Service members in the Federal government.[215],[216]

---

213 Johnsen, Mathiesen, and Gaup Eira, "Sami reindeer governance in Norway."

214 Paul Kivel, *Uprooting racism: How white people can work for racial justice* (Gabriola Island, BC: New Society Press, 1996), 19.

215 Richie Zweigenhaft, "Fortune 500 CEOs, 2000-2020: Still Male, Still White," The Society Pages, Department of Sociology at the University of Minnesota, October 28, 2020. Building Movement Project, Race to Lead: Confronting the Nonprofit Racial Leadership Gap (New York: Race to Lead Initiative, 2017), 1.

216 Brandon Lardy, "A revealing look at racial diversity in the federal government," *Fed Figures* (blog), We the Partnership, July 14, 2020.

ACKNOWLEDGMENTS

Thank you first and foremost to my friends and family, who support everything I do without end. *Welp* includes a lot of unpopular opinions, challenging stories, and incredibly personal reflections. No matter how emotionally difficult it might have been to read those, they committed to building the book you hold in your hands. Some early readers who deserve recognition include Treniyyah Anderson, Ashley Croker-Benn, Maria Boland, Lili Stith, Chandler Phillips, Andrea Lynne Oaks and Cynthia Zinakova.

In particular, I'd like to thank all of *Welp's* characters for taking the time to answer questions and provide content in these pages. Ole-Ante Turi, Ture-Biehtar Laiti, Michelle Saunders, Eben Hopson, Chilon Nyembwe and Matthildur Helgadóttir Jónudóttir not only provided their personal stories, but also established the intellectual basis for many of *Welp's* arguments. Those who remain unnamed have been equally brave and generous. *Giitu, tussen takk, takk takk, nakummek* and *quyanaq*.

Thanks are also due to the team at New Degree Press. *Skål* to Emily Price, my Managing Revisions Editor, for the care and effort she took in reviewing every chapter of this book.

Jemiscoe Chambers-Black, my developmental editor, seemed to glean the takeaways in my story drafts even before I did. *Welp* was a figment of my imagination back in 2018 and 2019, and New Degree Press is the main reason it has become a reality.

Moreover, I can hardly name all the people who made my experiences in Norway and Sápmi possible. Chief Gary Harrison and Cindy Dickson of Arctic Athabaskan Council, Anna Degteva of the Arctic Council Indigenous Peoples' Secretariat, and Alma Blount, Gunther Peck, and Lalita Kaligotla at Duke University's Hart Leadership Program deserve utmost thanks. At the Wilson Center's Polar Institute, Mike Sfraga's continued support of my vision is invaluable. The list of names goes on and on, because we can only achieve as much as other people invest in us.

I'd like to provide special recognition to all the people who supported my book before they even know what the pages might say. Without you, *Welp* would not have been possible (in no particular order):

Andrea Lynne Oaks	Michelle Saunders
Jo Ann Jones	Jack Durkee
Carol Stith	Eliza Moreno
Treniyyah Anderson	Chandler Phillips
Amanda King	Ivory Brown
Ambassador David Balton	Juanita Price
Nina Ågren	Anne Lott
Alma Blount	Naomi Lilly
Maria Boland	Anthony Ridges

Lou Kendaru

Marja Hætta

Emily Mills Ko

Arianna Carr

Nicole Eldred

Jasmine Henderson

Andrea Lynne Oaks

Chantal Reid, PhD

Sam Manzer

Amber Shearer

Ruth Nayeli Rivera

Sloan Talbot

Katie Taylor

Gloria Aldana

William A. Powers

Ayana Crawl-Bey

Kayo Bogdan

Kaia Pearson

Cynthia Zinakova

Baron Harper

Jasmine Hill

Colleen Fisk

Tara-Marie Desruisseaux

Emily A. Brockman

Karen A Ferguson, PhD

Jordan Peasant

Christy Lohr Sapp, PhD

Angie Griffe

Kimberly Aiken

Bryce Cracknell

Luke Farrell

Allen Pope, PhD

Helena Oaks

Riyanka Ganguly

Adrienne Hewitt

Jason M. Maher

Ruth Eckles

Jonathon Gillespie

Eboni Arrington

Judner Attys

Timothy Johnson, PhD

Maegan Seawright

Kristina Bär

Broderick Turner

Debbie George

Eric Koester

Dane Emmerling

Bryan Lockwood

Zoey Ferguson

David Malone, PhD

Anne Kathrine Utnes

Veronica Smith

Joël Plouffe, PhD

Michie Kawaoka

Marcie Keever

Rosa-Máren Magga

Antonio Lopez

Ashanti Smith-Watson

Anne Birgitte Hansen

Nadja Hipszer

Samantha Warren

Ryan Nilsen

Gianna Giordano

Tiffany Deguzman

The Honorable Sherri Goodman

Ginger Marshall

Ashley Croker-Benn

Mike Sfraga, PhD

Dylan Baffrey

Lili Stith

Malcolm Nowlin

Corey Pilson

Gudmundur Hjaltason

APPENDIX

AUTHOR'S NOTE

Aleut International Association, Arctic Athabaskan Council, Gwich'in Council International, Inuit Circumpolar Council, Russian Association of the Indigenous Peoples of the North, and The Saami Council. *VI Arctic Leaders' Summit Declaration*. Roavvenjárga: Arctic Council Indigenous Peoples' Secretariat, November 13 – 15, 2019.
https://static1.squarespace.com/static/58b6de9e414fb54d6c50134e/t/5dea325f736737
3ce5087580/1575629412149/Final+ALS6+and+ALYS+Declaration+%28secured%29.pdf.

America Counts (blog). "About 13.1 Percent Have a Master's, Professional Degree or Doctorate." February 19, 2010.
https://www.census.gov/library/stories/2019/02/number-of-people-with-masters-and-phd-degrees-double-since-2000.html#:~:text=Now%2C%20about%2013.1%20
percent%20of,Annual%20Social%20and%20Economic%20Supplement.

Garnett, Steven T., Neil D. Burgess, John E. Fa, Álvaro Fernández Llamazares, Zsolt Molnár, Cathy J. Robinson, and James E. M. Watson et al. "A spatial overview of the global importance of Indigenous lands for conservation." *Nature Sustainability* 1 (2018): 369–374.
https://www.nature.com/articles/s41893-018-0100-6.

Wills, Matthew. "Alaska's Unique Civil Rights Struggle." *JSTOR Daily*. March 26, 2018.
https://daily.jstor.org/alaskas-unique-civil-rights-struggle/.

CHAPTER 1

Alaska Eskimo Whaling Commission. "About Us." Accessed March 14, 2021.
http://www.aewc-alaska.org/about-us.html.

Beckmann-Dierkes, Norbert, and Johann C. Fuhrmann. *Immigration Country Norway—Demographic Trends and Political Concepts*. Berlin: Konrad-Adenauer-Stiftung, 2011.
https://www.kas.de/c/document_library/get_file?uuid=7ee7fdcd-e6be-d604-38fd-e3b70d2ca322&groupId=252038.

Brooks, James. "Alaska's population drops for the 3rd year in a row." *Anchorage Dispatch News.* Updated January 9, 2020.
https://www.adn.com/alaska-news/2020/01/09/alaskas-population-drops-for-the-3rd-year-in-a-row/.

Coggin, Jon Dos Passos. "New report highlights Alaska's last five years of dramatic climate change." *ClimateWatch Magazine,* October 15, 2019.
https://www.climate.gov/news-features/understanding-climate/new-report-highlights-alaska%E2%80%99s-last-five-years-dramatic-climate.

Cornwall, Warren. "The average US family destroys a football field's worth of Arctic sea ice every 30 years." *Science Magazine,* November 3, 2016.
https://www.sciencemag.org/news/2016/11/average-us-family-destroys-football-fields-worth-arctic-sea-ice-every-30-years?utm_source=newsfromscience&utm_medium=twitter&utm_campaign=seaice-8831.

Department of Revenue. *Spring 2014 Revenue Sources Book.* State of Alaska, 2014.
http://www.tax.alaska.gov/programs/documentviewer/viewer.aspx?1048r.

George, Kavitha. "Early data shows Alaska suicide rate stays constant, overdose rates increase." Alaska Public Media, December 23, 2020.
https://www.alaskapublic.org/2020/12/23/early-data-shows-alaska-suicide-rate-staying-constant-overdose-rate-increasing/.

Lukin, Maija. "Arctic Resilience Forum: Broadband Connectivity." Lecture at the virtual Arctic Resilience Forum, November 11, 2020.
https://www.wilsoncenter.org/event/arctic-resilience-forum-broadband-connectivity

Medred, Craig. "The deadliest state of all." *Anchorage Daily News.* Updated September 27, 2016.
https://www.adn.com/features/article/deadliest-state-all/2011/06/01/#:~:text=Alaska%20is%20now%20one%20of,of%20between%2054%20and%2057.

National Center for Health Statistics. "Firearm Mortality by State." Centers for Disease Control and Prevention. Last reviewed January 7, 2021.
https://www.cdc.gov/nchs/pressroom/sosmap/firearm_mortality/firearm.htm.

Nilsen, Thomas. "Expansion of Tromsø's Fram Centre makes room for more Arctic research cooperation." *The Barents Observer,* August 24, 2018.
https://thebarentsobserver.com/en/arctic/2018/08/fram-centre-opens-expanded-room-arctic-research.

O'Malley, Julia. *The Whale & the Cupcake: Stories of Subsistence, Longing and Community in Alaska.* Anchorage: Anchorage Museum, 2019.

O'Malley, Julia. "Whale hunting in Alaska: Point Hope, the village caught between tradition and climate change." *The Guardian,* July 16, 2015.
https://www.theguardian.com/travel/2015/jul/16/alaska-point-hope-whaling-climate.

Niche.com "2021 Most Diverse High Schools in America." Accessed January 9, 2021.
https://www.niche.com/k12/search/most-diverse-high-schools/.

Prison Policy Initiative. "Alaska profile." 2018.
https://www.prisonpolicy.org/profiles/AK.html.

Statistics Norway. "Immigrants and Norwegian-born to immigrant parents." March 9, 2020.
https://www.ssb.no/en/innvbef.

Simonelli, Isaac Stone. "Where Does All That Oil Go?" *Alaska Business Magazine*, October 2, 2018.
https://www.akbizmag.com/industry/oil-gas/where-does-all-that-oil-go/.

Standlea, David M. *Oil, Globalization, and the War for the Arctic Refuge.* Albany: State University of New York Press, 2006.

TemaNord, *SLiCA: Arctic Living Conditions—Living conditions and quality of life among, Inuit, Saami and indigenous peoples of Chukotka and the Kola Peninsula* (Copenhagen: Nordic Council of Ministers, 2015).
http://norden.diva-portal.org/smash/get/diva2:790312/FULLTEXT02.pdf.

Walker, Yaari. "Expansion of Maritime Activity in the Bering Strait Region: Mitigating Existing and Future Risks." Virtual lecture by the Wilson Center's Polar Institute, July 2020.
https://www.wilsoncenter.org/event/expansion-maritime-activity-bering-strait-region-mitigating-existing-and-future-risks.

World Population Review. "Anchorage, Alaska Population 2020." Accessed January 9, 2021.
https://worldpopulationreview.com/us-cities/anchorage-ak-population.

CHAPTER 2

Bourrelle, Julian S. "How to get to know Norwegians." *The Social Guidebook to Norway*, September 3, 2019.
https://www.thesocialguidebook.no/blogs/norwegian-culture/how-to-get-to-know-norwegians-2019.

Helgason, Haukur Már. "Iceland: The World's 4th Most Expensive Country." *The Reykjavik Grapevine*, January 22, 2015.
https://grapevine.is/news/2015/01/22/iceland-the-worlds-4th-most-expensive-country/.

How Widely Spoken. "How Widely Spoken is English in Norway?" Accessed January 10, 2021.
https://howwidelyspoken.com/how-widely-spoken-english-norway/.

Smith, David. "What's It Like to Work in Norway?" *A New Life in Trondheim* (blog). *Life in Norway*, March 2, 2015.
https://www.lifeinnorway.net/working-culture-norway/#:~:text=In%20Norway%2C%20employers%20are%20required,the%20average%20given%20to%20employees.

CHAPTER 3

22. juli-senteret. "The 22nd of July 2011." Accessed February 17, 2021.
https://22julisenteret.no/information-in-english/the-22nd-of-july-2011/.

Hansen, Kia Krarup, Turid Moldenæs, and Svein Disch Mathiesen. "The knowledge that went up in smoke: Reindeer herders' traditional knowledge of smoked reindeer meat in literature." *Polar Record* 55: 461.
https://www.cambridge.org/core/services/aop-cambridge-core/content/view/35E3039808D17362256A9BF1E6628967/S0032247420000170a.pdf/knowledge_that_went_up_in_smoke_reindeer_herders_traditional_knowledge_of_smoked_reindeer_meat_in_literature.pdf.

Hiss, Florian. "Tromsø as a 'Sámi Town'? – Language ideologies, attitudes, and debates surrounding bilingual language policies." *Language Policy* 12, no. 2 (May 2013): 177–196. https://link.springer.com/article/10.1007/s10993-012-9254-7.

Knightly, Philip. *Longtime Australian Policy: Kidnapping Children from Families.* London: The Center for Public Integrity, 2001. Updated 2014. https://publicintegrity.org/accountability/longtime-australian-policy-kidnapping-children-from-families/.

Minde, Henry. "The Norwegianization of the Sámi – why, how and what consequences?" Translated from Norwegian by Google. In *Sámi skuvlahistorjá 1*, edited by Svein Lund, Elfrid Boine, and Siri Broch Johansen. Kárášjohka/Karasjok: Davvi Girji, 2005. http://www.skuvla.info/skolehist/minde-n.htm.

Norwegian Ministry of Local Government and Modernisation. "The ILO Convention on the Rights of Indigenous Peoples." *Regjeringen*, February 20, 2020. https://www.regjeringen.no/en/topics/indigenous-peoples-and-minorities/urfolkryddemappe/the-ilo-convention-on-the-rights-of-indi/id487963/.

Museum for Northern Peoples. "Riddu Riđđu." Center for Northern Peoples, 9144 Samuelsberg, Norway. Accessed July 11, 2018 (in person).

Museum for Northern Peoples. "Svartskogen." Center for Northern Peoples, 9144 Samuelsberg, Norway. Accessed July 17, 2018 (in person).

Museum for Northern Peoples. "The Surveyor Case." Center for Northern Peoples, 9144 Samuelsberg, Norway. Accessed July 17, 2018 (in person).

Riddu Riđđu Festivála. "About Riddu Riđđu." Accessed January 10, 2021. https://riddu.no/en/about-riddu-riddu.

Sámisk Veivisare. "About Sámi Pathfinders." Accessed February 22, 2021. https://Sámiskeveivisere.no/en/about-Sámi-pathfinders/.

United Nations Regional Information Centre for Western Europe. "The Sámi of Northern Europe – one people, four countries." Accessed January 10, 2021. https://archive.unric.org/en/indigenous-people/27307-the-Sámi-of-northern-europe--one-people-four-countries.

Woodward, Kimmi. "The Sámi vs. Outsiders." *Sámi Culture* (blog), The University of Texas at Austin. Accessed January 10, 2021.

CHAPTER 4

Bertrand, Marianne, and Sendhil Mullainathan. "Are Emily and Greg More Employable Than Lakisha and Jamal? A Field Experiment on Labor Market Discrimination." *The American Economic Review* 94, no. 4 (2004): 991-1013. https://www.aeaweb.org/articles?id=10.1257/0002828042002561.

Bialik, Kristen. "For the fifth time in a row, the new Congress is the most racially and ethnically diverse ever." *FactTank* (blog). Pew Research Center, February 8, 2019. https://www.pewresearch.org/fact-tank/2019/02/08/for-the-fifth-time-in-a-row-the-new-congress-is-the-most-racially-and-ethnically-diverse-ever/.

McGee, Ny. "Fat Joe Talks Africa, Culture and Declares That 'Latinos Are Black.'" Electronic Urban Report/EUR. September 22, 2019. https://eurweb.com/2019/09/22/fat-joe-talks-africa-culture-and-says-latinos-are-black-watch/.

Sandset, Tony. *Color that Matters: A Comparative Approach to Mixed Race Identity and Nordic Exceptionalism*. New York: Routledge, 2020.

Young, Damon. "The Definition, Danger and Disease of Respectability Politics, Explained." *The Root*, March 21, 2016. https://www.theroot.com/the-definition-danger-and-disease-of-respectability-po-1790854699.

CHAPTER 5

2020 Proposed General Government Operating Budget (Anchorage: Municipality of Anchorage, 2020). https://www.muni.org/Departments/budget/operatingBudget/2020%20GGUB/2020%20Ppsd%20GGUB/WEB%20-%20Complete%20GGUB%20Book.pdf.

ArchCity Defenders, Ascend STL Inc., Metropolitan St. Louis Equal Housing and Opportunity Council (EHOC), Empower Missouri, *For the Sake of All* (Health Equity Works), Invest STL, and Team TIF. *Segregation in St. Louis: Dismantling the Divide*. St. Louis: Washington University in St. Louis, 2018. https://healthequityworks.wustl.edu/items/segregation-in-st-louis-dismantling-the-divide/.

Anderson, Carol. *White Rage: The Unspoken Truth of Our Racial Divide*. New York: Bloomsbury Publishing, 2016.

Bell, Jasmine. "5 Things to Know About Communities of Color and Environmental Justice." *Race and Ethnicity* (blog), Center for American Progress, April 25, 2016. https://www.americanprogress.org/issues/race/news/2016/04/25/136361/5 things to know-about-communities-of-color-and-environmental-justice/.

Davis, Angela Y. *Are Prisons Obsolete?* New York: Seven Stories Press, 2003.

Hartman, Ian C. "'Bonanza for Blacks?' Limits and Opportunities for African Americans in Southcentral Alaska." In *Imagining Anchorage: The Making of America's Northernmost Metropolis*, edited by James K. Barnett and Ian C. Hartman, 359-360. Fairbanks: University of Alaska Press, 2018.

New York Law School Racial Justice Project. "Unshared Bounty: How Structural Racism Contributes to the Creation and Persistence of Food Deserts (with American Civil Liberties Union)." Racial Justice Project, Book 3 (2012). https://digitalcommons.nyls.edu/cgi/viewcontent.cgi?article=1002&context=racial_justice_project.

PBS. "Lynching in America." *American Experience*. Accessed March 28, 2021. https://www.pbs.org/wgbh/americanexperience/features/emmett-lynching-america/.

Ruge, Edmund. "Black Self-determination Drawn From Our Roots." *Peripheries Journal* no. 5 (2020). https://revistaperiferias.org/en/materia/black-self-determination-drawn-from-our-roots/.

Starkley, Michael. "Wilderness, Race, and African Americans: An Environmental History from Slavery to Jim Crow." Master's thesis, University of California Berkeley, 2005. http://citeseerx.ist.psu.edu/viewdoc/download?doi=10.1.1.562.5468&rep=rep1&type=pdf.

Statistica Research Department. "Distribution of US millionaires by race/ethnicity, as of 2013." Statistica. Accessed February 24, 2020.

Statistica Research Department. "Countries with the Largest Number of Prisoners, as of June 2020." Statistica, December 1, 2020. https://www.statista.com/statistics/262961/countries-with-the-most-prisoners/.

Wills, Matthew. "Alaska's Unique Civil Rights Struggle." *JSTOR Daily*, March 26, 2018. https://daily.jstor.org/alaskas-unique-civil-rights-struggle/.

CHAPTER 6

Alaska Department of Fish and Game. "Regulations." Accessed February 28, 2021. http://www.adfg.alaska.gov/index.cfm?adfg=regulations.main.

Division of Subsistence. *Subsistence in Alaska: A Year 2017 Update*. Anchorage: Alaska Department of Fish & Game, 2018. https://www.adfg.alaska.gov/static/home/subsistence/pdfs/subsistence_update_2017.pdf.

Dunbar-Ortiz, Roxanne. "Excerpt: An Indigenous Peoples' History of the United States." Beacon Press. Accessed April 16, 2021. http://www.beacon.org/An-Indigenous-Peoples-History-of-the-United-States-P1164.aspx.

Hodgdon, Deenaalee and Haliehana Stepetin. "Xilegg I. Mapping: Accessing Indigenous Belonging to Place w/ Haliehana Stepetin." November 30, 2020. In *On The Land: Stories from the People, Stories from the Land*. In *How to Do Everything*. Produced by Deenaalee Hodgdon. Podcast, MP3 audio, 24:00-40:00. https://www.listennotes.com/podcasts/on-the-land/xilegg-i-mapping-accessing-8c1xItl6W2q/.

Encyclopaedia Britannica Online, Academic ed., s.v. "Norway: Health and Welfare," accessed March 20, 2021. https://www.britannica.com/place/Norway/Health-and-welfare.

Finney, Carolyn. *Black Faces, White Spaces: Reimagining the Relationship of African Americans to the Great Outdoors*. Chapel Hill: The University of North Carolina Press, 2014.

Worm, Boris, Edward B. Barbier, Nicola Beaumont, J. Emmett Duffy, Carl Folke, Benjamin S. Halpern, and Jeremy B. C. Jackson et al. "Impacts of Biodiversity Loss on Ocean Ecosystem Services," *Science* 314 no. 5800 (2006): 787-790. https://science.sciencemag.org/content/314/5800/787.

IUCN. "IUCN Director General's Statement on International Day of the World's Indigenous Peoples 2019." August 9, 2019. https://www.iucn.org/news/secretariat/201908/iucn-director-generals-statement-international-day-worlds-indigenous-peoples-2019.

Kalifornsky, Peter, and Katherine McNamara. *From the First Beginning, When the Animals Were Talking: On the Writing and Thought of Peter Kalifornsky*. Apple Books. Accessed February 20, 2021. http://artistsproofeditions.com/from-the-first-beginning/.

Native Peoples Action. "An Indigenous Vision for Our Collective Future: Becoming Earth's Stewards Again." *Nonprofit Quarterly* (Fall 2020). https://nonprofitquarterly.org/an-indigenous-vision-for-our-collective-future-becoming-earths-stewards-again/.

OpenBible.info. "100 Bible Verses about Buying Land." Accessed February 28, 2021. https://www.openbible.info/topics/buying_land.

Spence, Mark David. *Dispossessing the Wilderness: Indian Removal and the Making of the National Parks.* Oxford: Oxford University Press, 2000.

Starkley, Michael. "Wilderness, Race, and African Americans: An Environmental History from Slavery to Jim Crow." Master's thesis, University of California Berkeley, 2005. http://citeseerx.ist.psu.edu/viewdoc/download?doi=10.1.1.562.5468&rep=rep1&type=pdf.

Young, Oran R., D.G. Webster, Michael E. Cox, Jesper Raakjær, Lau Øfjord Blaxekjær, Níels Einarsson, and Ross A. Virginia et al. "Moving beyond panaceas in fisheries governance." *Proceedings of the National Academy of Sciences* 115, no. 37 (2018): 9065-9073. https://www.pnas.org/content/115/37/9065.

CHAPTER 7

American Road and Transportation Builders Association. "Bridge Report." Last updated March 11, 2021. https://artbabridgereport.org/.

Americans for Tax Fairness. "Fact Sheet: Taxing Wealthy Americans." 2014. https://americansfortaxfairness.org/tax-fairness-briefing-booklet/fact-sheet-taxing-wealthy-americans/.

Brooks, James. "Ferries on the chopping block and cuts to Pioneer Homes: A rundown of how Gov. Dunleavy's budget cuts would affect Alaskans." *Anchorage Daily News*, February 13, 2019. https://www.adn.com/politics/alaska-legislature/2019/02/14/ferries-on-the-chopping-block-and-cuts-to-pioneer-homes-a-rundown-of-how-gov-dunleavys-budget-cuts-would-affect-alaskans/.

Cole, Dermot. "How Norway and Alaska took different paths when it came to investing windfalls from oil development." *ArcticToday*, March 10, 2018. https://www.arctictoday.com/norway-alaska-took-different-paths-came-investing-windfalls-oil-development/.

CustomWeather. "Climate & Weather Averages in Tromsø, Norway." Time and Date AS. Accessed February 25, 2021. https://www.timeanddate.com/weather/norway/tromso/climate.

Danish Meteorological Institute. "Arctic +80 North Temperature." Accessed February 25, 2021. http://ocean.dmi.dk/arctic/meant80n_anomaly.uk.php.

Darity, William A., and A. Kirsten Mullen. *From Here to Equality: Reparations for Black Americans in the Twenty-First Century.* Chapel Hill: The University of North Carolina Press, 2020.

Denchak, Melissa. "Paris Climate Agreement: Everything You Need to Know." National Resource Defense Council, January 15, 2021. https://www.nrdc.org/stories/paris-climate-agreement-everything-you-need-know.

Department of Environmental Conservation, Division of Water. "Alaska Water and Sewer Challenge (AWSC)." Accessed March 24, 2021. https://dec.alaska.gov/water/water-sewer-challenge/.

Dunham, Will. "Scientists have figured out just how cold the last Ice Age was. Here's why it matters." *Global Agenda* (blog). World Economic Forum, September 1, 2020. https://www.weforum.org/agenda/2020/09/last-ice-age-global-temperature-scientist-predict#:~:text=The%20average%20global%20temperature%20during,than%202019%2C%20the%20researchers%20said.

Gore, Tim. "Confronting Carbon Inequality: Putting Climate Justice at the Heart of the COVID-19 Recovery." Oxfam Media Briefing, September 21, 2020. https://oxfamilibrary.openrepository.com/bitstream/handle/10546/621052/mb-confronting-carbon-inequality-210920-en.pdf?sequence=1&isAllowed=y.

Hou, Chia-Yi. "Alaska Governor Cuts $130 Million for University of Alaska System." *The Scientist*, July 1, 2019. https://www.the-scientist.com/news-opinion/alaska-governor-cuts-130-million-for-university-of-alaska-system-66064.

Linden, Michael. "What could the US afford if it raised billionaires' taxes? We do the math." *The Guardian*, December 13, 2019. https://www.theguardian.com/us-news/2019/dec/13/billionaires-taxes-inequality-one-percent.

Malmo, Vilde Kristine. "Ekstraordinært vær i nord: 30 grader og tropenatt." NRK/NTB. July 16, 2018. https://www.nrk.no/tromsogfinnmark/_-ekstraordinaert-vaer-i-nord_-30-grader-og-tropenatt-1.14129191.

Municipality of Anchorage. *Climate Action Plan.* Anchorage: Municipality of Anchorage, 2019. https://www.muni.org/departments/mayor/aware/resilientanchorage/documents/2019%20anchorage%20climate%20action%20plan_adopted.pdf.

Savage, Maddy. "What the Nordic nations can teach us about liveable cities." *Worklife* (blog). BBC, November 12, 2019. https://www.bbc.com/worklife/article/20191112-what-the-nordic-nations-can-teach-us-about-liveable-cities.

Statistica. "Distribution of US millionaires by race/ethnicity, as of 2013." Accessed February 24, 2020. https://www.statista.com/statistics/300528/us-millionaires-race-ethnicity/.

CHAPTER 8

Davis, Angela. *Are Prisons Obsolete?* New York: Seven Cities Press, 2003.

Ford, Aurora. "Redlining in Fairview." *Anchorage Press.* February 27, 2017. https://www.anchoragepress.com/news/redlining-in-fairview/article_cb0037a0-f9a7-11e6-b9eb-5fef409ab819.html.

Sandset, Tony. *Color that Matters: A Comparative Approach to Mixed Race Identity and Nordic Exceptionalism.* New York: Routledge, 2019.

Scandikitchen Blomhoj. "The Law of Jante—Explained." *ScandiKitchen* (blog). Accessed March 21, 2021. https://www.scandikitchen.co.uk/the-law-of-jante-explained/.

Statewide Suicide Prevention Council. "Alaska Suicide Facts and Statistics." Anchorage: Alaska Department of Health and Social Services. Accessed February 28, 2021. http://dhss.alaska.gov/suicideprevention/documents/pdfs_sspc/aksuicidestatistics.pdf.

Taking Action Against Racism in the Media. "Internalized Racism." October 17, 2016. https://www.div17.org/TAAR/media/topics/internalized-racism.php.

CHAPTER 9

Bangstad, Sindre. "The Racism that Dares not Speak its Name." *Intersections. East European Journal of Society and Politics* 1 (2015): 49 65. https://www.ceeol.com/search/article-detail?id=427360.

Ivory, Michael J. "To be anti-racist, Duke must get to the root of the matter." *Duke Magazine* (winter 2020 edition), December 8, 2020. https://alumni.duke.edu/magazine/articles/be-anti-racist-duke-must-get-root-matter.

Murison, Malek. "A Guide to Tromsø." Norway Travel Guide. Accessed March 28, 2021. https://norwaytravelguide.no/city-guides/a-guide-to-tromsoe

CHAPTER 10

Arnaquq-Bari, Alethea. *Angry Inuk*. Toronto: Unikkaat Studios, National Film Board of Canada & EyeSteelFilm, 2016. Vimeo rental. https://vimeo.com/ondemand/angryinuk.

Hellerstein, Erica, and Ken Fine. "A Million Tons of Feces and an Unbearable Stench: Life Near Industrial Pig Farms." *The Guardian,* September 20, 2017. https://www.theguardian.com/us-news/2017/sep/20/north-carolina-hog-industry-pig-farms.

Leahy, Stephen. "Choosing Chicken Over Beef Cuts Our Carbon Footprints a Surprising Amount." *National Geographic,* June 10, 2019. https://www.google.com/amp/s/api.nationalgeographic.com/distribution/public/amp/environment/2019/06/choosing-chicken-over-beef-cuts-carbon-footprint-surprising amount.

Lewis, Simon L., and Mark A. Maslin. "Defining the Anthropocene." *Nature* 519, no. 7542 (March 2015): 171–180. https://www.nature.com/articles/nature14258.

NC Pork Council. "Pork as a Passport: Food Unites Us." Accessed January 2, 2021. https://www.ncpork.org/exports/.

Yale School of Forestry & Environmental Studies. "Soy Agriculture in the Amazon Basin." *Global Forest Atlas*. Accessed January 2, 2021. https://globalforestatlas.yale.edu/amazon/land-use/soy.

CHAPTER 11

61/295. United Nations Declaration on the Rights of Indigenous Peoples (New York: United Nations, 2008). https://www.un.org/esa/socdev/unpfii/documents/DRIPS_en.pdf.

Alaska Department of Fish & Game. "Home." Accessed February 2, 2021. https://www.adfg.alaska.gov/index.cfm?adfg=home.main.

Buljo, Máret Rávdná, Andrei Dubovtsev, Rávdná Biret Márjá Eira Sara, Inger Marie Gaup Eira, Olga Fefelova, Kia Krarup Hansen, and Alexander Krasavin et al. "Sámi: Smoked & Cooked" in EALLU: *Indigenous Youth, Food Knowledge & Arctic Change.* Edited by Philip Burgess. Guovdageaidnu/Kautokeino: International Centre for Reindeer Husbandry, 2017. Print.

Gáldu - Resource Centre for Rights of Indigenous Peoples. "From Norwegianisation to Sámi movement - Recent history." Video, 0:00-0:30. Mar 30, 2007. https://youtu.be/QrgOA97wdZA.

Gaup Eira, Inger Marie, Anders Oskal, Inger Hanssen-Bauer, and Svein Disch Mathiesen. "Snow cover and the loss of traditional indigenous knowledge." *Nature Climate Change* 8 (November 2018): 924–936. https://www.researchgate.net/publication/328582027_Snow_cover_and_the_loss_ of_traditional_indigenous_knowledge.

Grande, Tove Rømo. "The Norwegian Government Ordered Massive Slaughterings of reindeer. Indigenous Sámi Reindeer Herders Disagreed But Were Not Heard." Norwegian University of Life Sciences, February 25, 2020. https://partner.sciencenorway.no/government-indigenous-people-nmbu/the-norwegian-government-ordered-massive-slaughterings-of-reindeer-indigenous-Sámi-reindeer-herders-disagreed-but-were-not-heard/1644157#:~:text=2020%20 %2D%2011%3A13-,For%20more%20than%20a%20decade%20the%20Norwegian%20 Government%20has%20implemented,of%20nearly%2040%20000%20reindeer.

International Centre for Reindeer Husbandry. "Sámi - Norway." Accessed February 3, 2021. https://reindeerherding.org/Sámi-norway.

Johnsen, Kathrine Ivsett, Svein Disch Mathiesen, and Inger Marie Gaup Eira. "Sámi reindeer governance in Norway as competing knowledge systems: a participatory study." *Ecology and Society* 22, no. 4 (2017): 33. https://www.ecologyandsociety.org/vol22/iss4/art33/#knowledge.

Marjomaa, Marko. *North Sámi in Norway: An Overview of a Language in Context* (Mainz: European Language Diversity for All (ELDIA), 2012). https://www.oulu.fi/sites/default/files/content/Giellagas_Marjomaa_ NorthSámiInNorway.pdf.

Minde, Henry. "Assimilation of the Sámi - Implementation and Consequences." Ontario: Aboriginal Policy Research Consortium International, 2005. https://ir.lib.uwo.ca/cgi/viewcontent.cgi?referer=& httpsredir=1&article=1248&context=aprci.

Samer.se. "Reindeer meat - a part of nature and Sámi culture." Accessed March 29, 2021. http://www.samer.se/4557.

CHAPTER 12

Arctic Council Indigenous Peoples' Secretariat, *Permanent Participant Panel at the UArctic Congress, September 2018 "Education and training in the Arctic: Identifying education and training needs for Arctic Indigenous Peoples"* (Tromsø: Arctic Council Open Access Archive, 2018). https://oaarchive.arctic-council.org/handle/11374/2248.

Briggs, Chad M. "Science, local knowledge and exclusionary practices: Lessons from the Alta Dam case." *Norsk Geografisk Tidsskrift - Norwegian Journal of Geography* 60, no. 2 (2006): 149-160.
https://www.tandfonline.com/doi/
abs/10.1080/00291950600723146?scroll=top&needAccess=true&journalCode=sgeo20.

Gathii, James Thuo. "Without Centering Race, Identity, and Indigeneity, Climate Responses Miss the Mark." In *21st Century Diplomacy: Foreign Policy is Climate Policy,* edited by Alexander Carius, Noah Gordon, and Lauren Risi (Washington, DC: Wilson Center and adelphi research gGmbH, 2020).
https://www.wilsoncenter.org/sites/default/files/media/uploads/documents/21st_
century_diplomacy_report_spread.pdf.

Johnsen, Kathrine Ivsett. "Conflicting knowledges, competing worldviews: Norwegian governance of Sámi reindeer husbandry in West Finnmark, Norway." Doctoral thesis, Norwegian University of Life Sciences, Ås, 2018.

Johnsen, Kathrine Ivsett. "The paradox of reindeer pasture management in Finnmark, Norway." Strategic Environmental Impact Assessment of Development of the Arctic. September 2014.
https://www.arcticinfo.eu/en/features/112 the paradox of reindeer-pasture-management-in-finnmark-norway.

Kiersz, Andy. "The 15 US states with the lowest college graduation rates." *Business Insider,* June 7, 2019.
https://www.businessinsider.com/us-states-with-the-lowest-college-graduation-rates-2019-6.

Lawrence, William. "Saami and Norwegians protest construction of Alta Dam, Norway, 1979-1981." Global Nonviolent Action Database. January 30, 2011.
https://nvdatabase.swarthmore.edu/content/saami-and-norwegians-protest-construction-alta-dam-norway-1979-1981.

McGwin, Kevin. "Reindeer herders say they will sue to halt Norway's largest wind farm." *ArcticToday,* July 1, 2020.
https://www.arctictoday.com/reindeer-herders-say-they-will-sue-to-halt-to-norways-largest-wind-farm/.

Nilsen, Thomas. "How miners' hunt for metals to power electric cars threatens Sámi reindeer herders' homeland." *ArcticToday,* July 13, 2020.
https://www.arctictoday.com/how-miners-hunt-for-metals-to-power-electric-cars-threatens-Sámi-reindeer-herders-homeland.

Nilsen, Thomas. "Norway greenlights copper mine with tailings to be dumped in Arctic fjord." *The Barents Observer,* November 30, 2019.
https://thebarentsobserver.com/en/industry-and-energy/2019/11/norway-greenlights-copper-mine-tailings-dump-arctic-fjord.

Nilsen, Thomas. "The dream of an Arctic railway fades as Sámi herders signal 'veto.'" *ArcticToday,* March 5, 2020.
https://www.arctictoday.com/the-dream-of-an-arctic-railway-fades-as-Sámi-herders-signal-veto/.

Public School Review. "Top Graduation Rate Public Schools in Alaska." Accessed March 5, 2021.
https://www.publicschoolreview.com/graduation-rate-stats/
alaska#:~:text=Public%20school%20in%20Alaska%20achieve,of%2077%25%20(2021).

Stith, Michaela. "Big ships welcomed at the Arctic Circle conference." *Friends of the Earth* (blog). Medium, December 22, 2016. https://medium.com/oceans-vessels/big-ships-welcomed-at-the-arctic-circle-conference-63eb0aef5912.

Strzyżyńska, Weronika. "Sámi reindeer herders file lawsuit against Norway windfarm." *The Guardian*, January 18, 2021. https://www.theguardian.com/world/2021/jan/18/Sámi-reindeer-herders-file-lawsuit-against-oyfjellet-norway-windfarm-project.

Turi, Johan Mathis. "Native reindeer herders' priorities for research." *Polar Research* 19, no. 1 (January 2000): 131-133. https://doi.org/10.3402/polar.v19i1.6539.

CHAPTER 13

Arctic Research Consortium of the United States. "12 – Melting Ice & Thawing Permafrost." September 23, 2019. Panel at Arctic Futures 2050, 9:00-11:45. Featuring Maija Lukin. https://www.youtube.com/watch?v=PEWHFx0950g.

Arctic Research Consortium of the United States. "After the Ice - Part 1: Our Food." October 7, 2020. Video, 7:34. https://www.youtube.com/watch?v=1enqXQ1A0M4.

Arctic Research Consortium of the United States, "Arctic Futures 2050 Conference: Day 2," September 5, 2015. Video, 12:13-14:24. Featuring Maija Lukin. https://www.youtube.com/watch?v=KUvz9H7PPn8.

Durand, Kristen. "Data shows youth suicide is higher in Alaska." *Alaska's News Source*, October 3, 2020. https://www.alaskasnewssource.com/2020/10/04/data-shows-youth-suicide-is-higher-in-alaska/.

Eben Hopson Memorial Archives. "A Short Biography on the Honorable Eben Hopson." Accessed February 6, 2021. http://ebenhopson.com/biography/.

FAO and FILAC. *Forest governance by indigenous and tribal peoples. An opportunity for climate action in Latin America and the Caribbean.* Santiago: FAO, 2021. http://www.fao.org/3/cb2953en/cb2953en.pdf.

Fleischer, N.L., P. Melstrom, E. Yard, M. Brubaker, and T. Thomas. "The epidemiology of falling-through-the-ice in Alaska, 1990–2010." *Journal of Public Health* 36, no. 2 (June 2014): 235–242. https://academic.oup.com/jpubhealth/article/36/2/235/1548603.

Hansen, Terry. "More People Are Falling Through the Arctic's Melting Ice Never to Be Seen Again." *Motherboard: Tech by Vice* (blog). Vice Media Group, September 16, 2019. https://www.vice.com/en/article/qvgjxw/more-people-are-falling-through-the-arctics-melting-ice-never-to-be-seen-again.

Intergovernmental Panel on Climate Change (IPCC). "Special Report on the Ocean and Cryosphere in a Changing Climate (SROCC): Chapter 3, Polar Regions." Accessed March 24, 2021. https://www.ipcc.ch/srocc/chapter/chapter-3-2/.

McGwin, Kevin. "Sámi herders fear supplementary feeding is changing the nature of their livelihood." *ArcticToday*, February 11, 2021. https://www.arctictoday.com/Sámi-herders-fear-supplementary-feeding-is-changing-the-nature-of-their-livelihood/.

Hensley, William L. Iggiagruk. *Fifty Miles from Tomorrow: A Memoir of Alaska and the Real People*. New York: Picador, 2009.

Inuit Circumpolar Council. "About ICC." Accessed February 7, 2021. https://www.inuitcircumpolar.com/about-icc/

Inuit Circumpolar Council Alaska. *Alaskan Inuit Food Security Conceptual Framework: How to Assess the Arctic from an Inuit Perspective*. Anchorage: ICC Alaska, 2016. https://iccalaska.org/wp-icc/wp-content/uploads/2016/03/Food-Security-Report-Brochure.pdf.

Kuokkanen, Rauna. "Indigenous Economies, Theories of Subsistence, and Women: Exploring the Social Economy Model for Indigenous Governance." *American Indian Quarterly* 35, no. 2 (Spring 2011): 215–240. https://www.jstor.org/stable/10.5250/amerindiquar.35.2.0215?seq=1.

Northern Alaska Sea Ice Project Jukebox. "Roy and Savik Ahmaogak, Part 1." Digital Branch of the University of Alaska Fairbanks Oral History Program. June 1, 2017. https://jukebox.uaf.edu/site7/interviews/2950

Peak Three. "People of the Ice Whale." Video, 9:44. https://www.peakthree.com/work/.

Pettinger, Tejvan. "Externalities—definition." *Economics Help* (blog). Accessed March 7, 2021. https://www.economicshelp.org/blog/glossary/externalities/.

Robertscribbler (blog). "10 15 Foot Waves Break Seawall at Barrow, Alaska." Dark Forest Press, August 27, 2015. https://robertscribbler.com/2015/08/27/ten-foot-waves-break-seawall-at-barrow-alaska/.

Statewide Suicide Prevention Council. "Alaska Suicide Facts and Statistics." Anchorage: Alaska Department of Health and Social Services. Accessed February 28, 2021. http://dhss.alaska.gov/suicideprevention/documents/pdfs_sspc/aksuicidestatistics.pdf.

Stuhl, Andrew. *Unfreezing the Arctic: Science, Colonialism, and the Transformation of Inuit Lands*. Chicago: University of Chicago Press, 2016.

University of Alaska Anchorage. "Kiuguyat: The Northern Lights." Accessed March 22, 2021. https://www.uaa.alaska.edu/academics/college-of-arts-and-sciences/programs/planetarium/kiuguyat.cshtml.

Wollan, Malia. "How to Herd Reindeer." *New York Times*, February 11, 2020. https://www.nytimes.com/2020/02/11/magazine/how-to-herd-reindeer.html.

CHAPTER 14

Bennett, Abbie. "Campus coffee shop was playing rap. Duke VP's complaint got employees fired, IndyWeek reports." *The News & Observer*, May 9, 2018. https://www.newsobserver.com/news/local/counties/durham-county/article210735884.html.

Kanyogo, Mumbi N. "Anonymous Anti-Blackness and Institutional Racism." In *Duke Disorientation Guide 2018*. September 9, 2018. https://issuu.com/dukedisorientationguide/docs/disorientationguide_finalfinal.

Ramakrishnan, Karthick. "'Strange' vs. 'simple old American' names." *The Chicago Tribune*, May 28, 2015. https://www.chicagotribune.com/la-oe-0528-ramakrishnan-duke-racist-names-20150528-story.html.

Svrluga, Susan. "Duke official apologizes for lack of 'civility' in parking dispute as sit-in over racial slur continues." Washington Post, April 4, 2016. https://www.washingtonpost.com/news/grade-point/wp/2016/04/04/duke-official-apologizes-for-lack-of-civility-in-parking-dispute-as-sit-in-over-racial-issues-continues/.

CHAPTER 15

Amnesty International Canada. "Black and Indigenous Solidarity Against Systemic Racism." *Human Rights Now* (blog), July 20, 2020. https://www.amnesty.ca/blog/black-and-indigenous-solidarity-against-systemic-racism.

Climate Justice Alliance. "Just Transition: A Framework for Change." Accessed March 28, 2021. https://climatejusticealliance.org/just-transition/.

Cook, Nicholas. *Conflict Minerals in Central Africa: US and International Responses*. Washington, DC: Congressional Research Service, 2012. https://fas.org/sgp/crs/row/R42618.pdf.

Encyclopaedia Britannica Online. Academic ed. s.v. "How did Patrice Lumumba die?" Accessed March 28, 2021. https://www.britannica.com/story/how-did-patrice-lumumba-die.

Google. "Happy Valley-Goose Bay, NL, Canada Weather averages." Accessed April 2, 2021. https://www.google.com/search?q=average+temperature+in+happy+valley+goose+bay&rlz=1C1CHBF_enUS858US861&oq=happy+valley+goose+bay+avrage+temp&aqs=chrome.1.69i57j0i22i30.11729j0j9&sourceid=chrome&ie=UTF-8.

National Geographic Resource Library, s.v. " Aurora." Last updated May 14, 2011. https://www.nationalgeographic.org/encyclopedia/aurora/#:~:text=In%20the%20ionosphere%2C%20the%20ions,miles)%20above%20the%20Earth's%20surface.

Native Peoples Action. "An Indigenous Vision for Our Collective Future: Becoming Earth's Stewards Again." *Nonprofit Quarterly* (Fall 2020). https://nonprofitquarterly.org/an-indigenous-vision-for-our-collective-future-becoming-earths-stewards-again/.

Nzongola-Ntalaja, Georges. "Patrice Lumumba: the most important assassination of the 20th century." *The Guardian*, January 17, 2011. https://www.theguardian.com/global-development/poverty-matters/2011/jan/17/patrice-lumumba-50th-anniversary-assassination.

Nzongola-Ntalaja, Georges. *The Congo from Leopold to Kabila: A People's History*. United Kingdom: Bloomsbury Academic, 2002.

Saunders, Michelle. "A Nunatsiavut Field Guide to the Birds of Labrador." Tradition and Transition. September 2018. https://traditionandtransition.com/stories/nunatsiavut-birds/.

The Woodrow Wilson International Center for Scholars' Cold War International History Project and Africa Program. *The Congo Crisis, 1960-1961: A Critical Oral History Conference*. Washington, DC: Woodrow Wilson International Center for Scholars, 2004.

Tradition and Transition. "Nunatsiavut." Accessed March 28, 2021. https://traditionandtransition.com/nunatsiavut/.

Weather Atlas. "February weather forecast and climate: Tromsø, Norway." Accessed February 17, 2021. https://www.weather-atlas.com/en/norway/tromso-weather-february#:~:text=In%20Troms%C3%B8%2C%20in%20February%2C%20the,C%20(40.3%C2%B0F).

EPILOGUE

22. juli-**senteret**. "The 22nd of July 2011." Accessed February 17, 2021. https://22julisenteret.no/information-in-english/the-22nd-of-july-2011/

Cowen, Richard. "US Capitol Police investigating role of 35 officers during January 6 riot." *Reuters*, February 19, 2021. https://www.reuters.com/article/us-usa-trump-capitol-police/u-s-capitol-police-investigating-role-of-35-officers-during-january-6-riot-idUSKBN2AJ243.

Greaves, Wilfred. "Cities and Human Security in a Warming Arctic." In *Climate Change and Arctic Security*. Edited by Lassi Heininen and Heather Exner-Pirot, 61-89. New York: Palgrave Pivot, 2020.

Kolås, Åshild. "How critical is the event? Multicultural Norway after 22 July 2011." *Taylor & Francis Online* 23, no. 5 (January 2017): 518-532. https://www.tandfonline.com/doi/full/10.1080/13504630.2016.1271740

Pape, Robert A., and Keven Ruby. "The Capitol Rioters Aren't Like Other Extremists." *The Atlantic*, February 2, 2021. https://www.theatlantic.com/ideas/archive/2021/02/the-capitol-rioters-arent-like-other-extremists/617895/.

Shane III, Leo. "Troops: White nationalism a national security threat equal to ISIS, al-Qaida." *Military Times*, September 3, 2020. https://www.militarytimes.com/news/pentagon-congress/2020/09/03/troops-white-nationalism-a-national-security-threat-equal-to-isis-al-qaeda/

Sonne, Paul, Peter Hermann, and Missy Ryan. "Pentagon placed limits on DC Guard ahead of pro-Trump protests due to narrow mission." *Washington Post*, January 7, 2021. https://www.washingtonpost.com/national-security/trump-protests-washington-guard-military/2021/01/07/c5299b56-510e-11eb-b2e8-3339e73d9da2_story.html.

UiT The Arctic University of Norway University Library. "Ságastallamin – Telling the story of Arctic Indigenous languages." Accessed April 2, 2021. https://site.uit.no/sagastallamin/.

Waldman, Paul. "Yes, Opposition to Obamacare is Tied Up with Race." *Plum Line* (blog). *Washington Post*, May 23, 2014. https://www.washingtonpost.com/blogs/plum-line/wp/2014/05/23/yes-opposition-to-obamacare-is-tied-up-with-race/.

GLOSSARY

Office of the High Commissioner on Human Rights. "2200A (XXI). International Covenant on Economic, Social and Cultural Rights." United Nations. Entered into force January 3, 1976. https://www.ohchr.org/EN/ProfessionalInterest/Pages/CESCR.aspx.

Arctic Council. "About the Arctic Council." Accessed March 28, 2021. https://arctic-council.org/en/about/.

Building Movement Project. *Race to Lead: Confronting the Nonprofit Racial Leadership Gap.* New York: Race to Lead Initiative, 2017. https://racetolead.org/wp-content/uploads/2017/12/RacetoLead_ExecutiveSummary-2.pdf.

Christmas-Rouse, Chandra, Brandon C. Jones, and Meghan Venable-Thomas. *Building to Heal: A Framework for Holistic Community Development.* Enterprise Community: December 2020. https://www.enterprisecommunity.org/resources/building-heal-framework-holistic-community-development-11471.

Kivel, Paul. *Uprooting racism: How white people can work for racial justice.* Gabriola Island, BC: New Society Press, 1996.

Johnsen, Kathrine Ivsett, Svein Disch Mathiesen, and Inger Marie Gaup Eira. "Sámi reindeer governance in Norway as competing knowledge systems: a participatory study." *Ecology and Society* 22, no. 4 (2017). https://www.ecologyandsociety.org/vol22/iss4/art33/#knowledge.

Jung, Martin, Pedram Rowhani, and Jörn P. W. Scharlemann. "Impacts of past abrupt land change on local biodiversity globally." *Nature Communications* 10, no. 5474 (2019). https://www.nature.com/articles/s41467-019-13452-3.

McKenna, Ryan. "The Wilson Center Once Again Named A Top 10 Think Tank Worldwide." Wilson Center press release. January 28, 2021. https://www.wilsoncenter.org/article/wilson-center-once-again-named-top-10-think-tank-worldwide.

Minde, Henry. "The Norwegianization of the Sámi - why, how and what consequences?" Translated from Norwegian by Google. In *Sámi skuvlahistorjá 1,* edited by Svein Lund, Elfrid Boine and Siri Broch Johansen. Kárášjohka/Karasjok: Davvi Girji, 2005. http://www.skuvla.info/skolehist/minde-n.htm.

ScienceDirect. "Land Use Change." Accessed March 11, 2021. https://www.sciencedirect.com/topics/earth-and-planetary-sciences/land-use-change.

Lardy, Brandon. "A revealing look at racial diversity in the federal government." *Fed Figures* (blog). We the Partnership, July 14, 2020. https://ourpublicservice.org/blog/a-revealing-look-at-racial-diversity-in-the-federal-government/.

UNFCCC Secretariat. "Land Use, Land-Use Change and Forestry." United Nations Climate Change. Accessed March 11, 2021. https://unfccc.int/topics/land-use/workstreams/land-use--land-use-change-and-forestry-lulucf/land-use--land-use-change-and-forestry.

United Nations Permanent Forum on Indigenous Issues. *Who are indigenous peoples?* Factsheet. Accessed March 12, 2021. https://www.un.org/esa/socdev/unpfii/documents/5session_factsheet1.pdf.

Wijeyesinghe, Charmaine L., Pat Griffin, and Barbara Love. "Racism-Curriculum Design." In *Teaching for Diversity and Social Justice*, edited by Maurianne Adams, Lee Anne Bell, and Pat Griffin, 88-99. New York: Routledge, 1997. https://www.vanderbilt.edu/oacs/wp-content/uploads/sites/140/Key-Terms-Racism.pdf.

Zweigenhaft, Richie. "Fortune 500 CEOs, 2000-2020: Still Male, Still White." The Society Pages. Department of Sociology at the University of Minnesota, October 28, 2020. https://thesocietypages.org/specials/fortune-500-ceos-2000-2020-still-male-still-white/.

CPSIA information can be obtained
at www.ICGtesting.com
Printed in the USA
LVHW080503300122
709678LV00014B/509